Library, Dinnington Campus
Rotherham College
Doe Quarry Lane, Dinnington, S25 2NF
Renewals/Enquiries: 01909 559279

0049410

Harper Press
An imprint of HarperCollins*Publishers*
77–85 Fulham Palace Road
Hammersmith
London W6 8JB

This Harper Press paperback edition published 2013

A catalogue record for this book is available from the British Library

ISBN: 978-0-00-792548-3

Printed and bound in Great Britain by Clays Ltd, St Ives plc

MIX
Paper from
responsible sources
FSC® **C007454**

FSC™ is a non-profit international organisation established to promote
the responsible management of the world's forests. Products carrying the
FSC label are independently certified to assure consumers that they come
from forests that are managed to meet the social, economic and
ecological needs of present and future generations,
and other controlled sources.

Find out more about HarperCollins and the environment at
www.harpercollins.co.uk/green

Life & Times section © Gerard Cheshire
Introduction by Philip Hobsbaum
Shakespeare: Words and Phrases adapted from
Collins English Dictionary
Typesetting in Kalix by Palimpsest Book Production Limited,
Falkirk, Stirlingshire

10 9 8 7 6 5 4 3 2 1

+
FEB 14
0049410
822.33 WIN

Prefatory Note

This Shakespeare play uses the full Alexander text. By keeping in mind the fact that the language has changed considerably in four hundred years, as have customs, jokes, and stage conventions, the editors have aimed at helping the modern reader – whether English is their mother tongue or not – to grasp the full significance of the play. The Notes, intended primarily for examination candidates, are presented in a simple, direct style. The needs of those unfamiliar with British culture have been specially considered.

Since quiet study of the printed word is unlikely to bring fully to life plays that were written directly for the public theatre, attention has been drawn to dramatic effects which are important in performance. The editors see Shakespeare's plays as living works of art which can be enjoyed today on stage, film and television in many parts of the world.

CONTENTS

An Elizabethan playhouse. Note the apron stage protruding into the auditorium, the space below it, the inner room at the rear of the stage, the gallery above the inner stage, the canopy over the main stage, and the absence of a roof over the audience.

The Theatre in Shakespeare's Day

On the face of it, the conditions in the Elizabethan theatre were not such as to encourage great writers. The public playhouse itself was not very different from an ordinary inn-yard; it was open to the weather; among the spectators were often louts, pickpockets and prostitutes; some of the actors played up to the rowdy elements in the audience by inserting their own jokes into the authors' lines, while others spoke their words loudly but unfeelingly; the presentation was often rough and noisy, with fireworks to represent storms and battles, and a table and a few chairs to represent a tavern; there were no actresses, so boys took the parts of women, even such subtle and mature ones as Cleopatra and Lady Macbeth; there was rarely any scenery at all in the modern sense. In fact, a quick inspection of the English theatre in the reign of Elizabeth I by a time-traveller from the twentieth century might well produce only one positive reaction: the costumes were often elaborate and beautiful.

Shakespeare himself makes frequent comments in his plays about the limitations of the playhouse and the actors of his time, often apologizing for them. At the beginning of *Henry V* the Prologue refers to the stage as 'this unworthy scaffold' and to the theatre building (the Globe, probably) as 'this wooden O', and emphasizes the urgent need for imagination in making up for all the deficiencies of presentation. In introducing Act IV the Chorus goes so far as to say:

> . . . we shall much disgrace
> With four or five most vile and ragged foils,
> Right ill-dispos'd in brawl ridiculous,
> The name of Agincourt, (lines 49–52)

In *A Midsummer Night's Dream* (Act V, Scene i) he seems to dismiss actors with the words:

The best in this kind are but shadows.

Yet Elizabeth's theatre, with all its faults, stimulated dramatists to a variety of achievement that has never been equalled and, in Shakespeare, produced one of the greatest writers in history. In spite of all his grumbles he seems to have been fascinated by the challenge that it presented him with. It is necessary to re-examine his theatre carefully in order to understand how he was able to achieve so much with the materials he chose to use. What sort of place was the Elizabethan playhouse in reality? What sort of people were these criticized actors? And what sort of audiences gave them their living?

The Development of the Theatre up to Shakespeare's Time

For centuries in England noblemen had employed groups of skilled people to entertain them when required. Under Tudor rule, as England became more secure and united, actors such as these were given more freedom, and they often performed in public, while still acknowledging their 'overlords' (in the 1570s, for example, when Shakespeare was still a schoolboy at Stratford, one famous company was called 'Lord Leicester's Men'). London was rapidly becoming larger and more important in the second half of the sixteenth century, and many of the companies of actors took the opportunities offered to establish themselves at inns on the main roads leading to the City (for example, the Boar's Head in Whitechapel and the Tabard in South-wark) or in the City itself. These groups of actors would come to an agreement with the inn-keeper which would give them the use of the yard for their performances after people had eaten and drunk well in the middle of the day. Before long, some inns were taken over completely by companies of players and thus became the first public theatres. In 1574 the officials of the City of London issued an order which shows clearly that these theatres were both popular and also offensive to some respectable people, because the order complains about 'the inordinate haunting of great multitudes of people, specially youth, to plays interludes and shows; namely occasion of frays and quarrels, evil practices of incontinency in great inns . . .' There is evidence that, on public holidays, the theatres on the banks of the Thames were crowded with noisy apprentices and tradesmen, but it would be wrong to think that audiences were always undiscriminating and loudmouthed. In spite of the disapproval of Puritans and the more staid members of society, by the 1590s, when Shakespeare's plays were beginning to be performed, audiences consisted of a good cross-section of English society, nobility as well as workers, intellectuals as well as simple people out for a laugh; also (and in this respect English theatres were unique in Europe), it was quite normal for respectable women to attend plays. So Shakespeare had to write plays which would appeal to people of widely different kinds. He had to provide 'something for everyone' but at the same time to take care to unify the material so that it would not seem to fall into separate pieces as they watched it. A speech like that of the drunken porter in *Macbeth* could provide the 'groundlings' with a belly-laugh, but also held a deeper significance for those who could appreciate it. The audience he wrote for was one of a number of apparent drawbacks which Shakespeare was able to turn to his and our advantage.

Shakespeare's Actors

Nor were all the actors of the time mere 'rogues, vagabonds and sturdy beggars' as some were described in a Statute of 1572. It is true that many of them had a hard life and earned very little money, but leading actors could become partners in the ownership of the theatres in which they acted: Shakespeare was a shareholder in the Globe and the Blackfriars theatres when he was an actor as well as a playwright. In any case, the attacks made on Elizabethan actors were usually directed at their morals and not at their acting ability; it is clear that many of them must have been good at their trade if they were able to interpret complex works like the great tragedies in such a way as to attract enthusiastic audiences. Undoubtedly some of the boys took the women's parts with skill and confidence, since a man called Coryate, visiting Venice in 1611, expressed surprise that women could act as well as they: 'I saw women act, a thing that I never saw before . . . and they performed it with as good a grace, action, gesture . . . as ever I saw any masculine actor.' The quality of most of the actors who first presented Shakespeare's plays is probably accurately summed up by Fynes Moryson, who wrote, '. . . as there be, in my opinion, more plays in London than in all the parts of the world I have seen, so do these players or comedians excel all other in the world.'

The Structure of the Public Theatre

Although the 'purpose-built' theatres were based on the inn-yards which had been used for play-acting, most of them were circular. The walls contained galleries on three storeys from which the wealthier patrons watched, they must have been something like the 'boxes' in a modern theatre, except that they held much larger numbers – as many as 1500. The 'groundlings' stood on the floor of the building, facing a raised stage which projected from the 'stage-wall', the main features of which were:

1 a small room opening on to the back of the main stage and on the same level as it (rear stage),
2 a gallery above this inner stage (upper stage),
3 canopy projecting from above the gallery over the main stage, to protect the actors from the weather (the 700 or 800 members of the audience who occupied the yard, or 'pit' as we call it today, had the sky above them).

In addition to these features there were dressing-rooms behind the stage and a space underneath it from which entrances could be made through trap-doors. All the acting areas – main stage, rear stage, upper stage and under stage – could be entered by actors directly from their dressing rooms, and all of them were used in productions of Shakespeare's plays. For example, the inner stage, an almost cavelike structure, would have been where Ferdinand and Miranda are 'discovered' playing chess in the last act of *The Tempest*, while the upper stage was certainly the balcony from which Romeo climbs down in Act III of *Romeo and Juliet*.

It can be seen that such a building, simple but adaptable, was not really unsuited to the presentation of plays like Shakespeare's. On the contrary, its simplicity guaranteed the minimum of distraction, while its shape and construction must have produced a sense of involvement on the part of the audience that modern producers would envy.

Other Resources of the Elizabethan Theatre

Although there were few attempts at scenery in the public theatre (painted backcloths were occasionally used in court performances), Shakespeare and his fellow playwrights were able to make use of a fair variety of 'properties', lists of such articles have survived: they include beds, tables, thrones, and also trees, walls, a gallows, a Trojan horse and a 'Mouth of Hell'; in a list of properties belonging to the manager, Philip Henslowe, the curious item 'two mossy banks' appears. Possibly one of them was used for the

> bank whereon the wild thyme blows,
> Where oxlips and the nodding violet grows

in *A Midsummer Night's Dream* (Act II, Scene i). Once again, imagination must have been required of the audience.

Costumes were the one aspect of stage production in which

trouble and expense were hardly ever spared to obtain a magnificent effect. Only occasionally did they attempt any historical accuracy (almost all Elizabethan productions were what we should call 'modern-dress' ones), but they were appropriate to the characters who wore them: kings were seen to be kings and beggars were similarly unmistakable. It is an odd fact that there was usually no attempt at illusion in the costuming: if a costume looked fine and rich it probably was. Indeed, some of the costumes were almost unbelievably expensive. Henslowe lent his company £19 to buy a cloak, and the Alleyn brothers, well-known actors, gave £20 for a 'black velvet cloak, with sleeves embroidered all with silver and gold, lined with black satin striped with gold'.

With the one exception of the costumes, the 'machinery' of the playhouse was economical and uncomplicated rather than crude and rough, as we can see from this second and more leisurely look at it. This meant that playwrights were stimulated to produce the imaginative effects that they wanted from the language that they used. In the case of a really great writer like Shakespeare, when he had learned his trade in the theatre as an actor, it seems that he received quite enough assistance of a mechanical and structural kind without having irksome restrictions and conventions imposed on him; it is interesting to try to guess what he would have done with the highly complex apparatus of a modern television studio. We can see when we look back to his time that he used his instrument, the Elizabethan theatre, to the full, but placed his ultimate reliance on the communication between his imagination and that of his audience through the medium of words. It is, above all, his rich and wonderful use of language that must have made play-going at that time a memorable experience for people of widely different kinds. Fortunately, the deep satisfaction of appreciating and enjoying Shakespeare's work can be ours also, if we are willing to overcome the language difficulty produced by the passing of time.

Shakespeare: A Timeline

Very little indeed is known about Shakespeare's private life; the facts included here are almost the only indisputable ones. The dates of Shakespeare's plays are those on which they were first produced.

1558 Queen Elizabeth crowned.

1561 Francis Bacon born.

1564 Christopher Marlowe born. William Shakespeare born, April 23rd, baptized April 26th.

1566 Shakespeare's brother, Gilbert, born.

1567 Mary, Queen of Scots, deposed.
James VI (later James I of England) crowned King of Scotland.

1572 Ben Jonson born.
Lord Leicester's Company (of players) licensed; later called Lord Strange's, then the Lord Chamberlain's and finally (under James) the King's Men.

1573 John Donne born.

1574 The Common Council of London directs that all plays and playhouses in London must be licensed.

1576 James Burbage builds the first public playhouse, The Theatre, at Shoreditch, outside the walls of the City.

1577 Francis Drake begins his voyage round the world (completed 1580).
Holinshed's Chronicles of England, Scotland and Ireland published (which

Shakespeare later used extensively).

1582		Shakespeare married to Anne Hathaway.
1583	The Queen's Company founded by royal warrant.	Shakespeare's daughter, Susanna, born.
1585		Shakespeare's twins, Hamnet and Judith, born.
1586	Sir Philip Sidney, the Elizabethan ideal 'Christian knight', poet, patron, soldier, killed at Zutphen in the Low Countries.	
1587	Mary, Queen of Scots, beheaded. Marlowe's *Tamburlaine (Part I)* first staged.	
1588	Defeat of the Spanish Armada. Marlowe's *Tamburlaine (Part II)* first staged.	
1589	Marlowe's *Jew of Malta* and Kyd's *Spanish Tragedy* (a 'revenge tragedy' and one of the most popular plays of Elizabethan times).	
1590	Spenser's *Faerie Queene* (Books I–III) published.	
1592	Marlowe's *Doctor Faustus* and *Edward II* first staged. Witchcraft trials in Scotland. Robert Greene, a rival playwright, refers to Shakespeare as 'an upstart crow' and 'the only Shake-scene in a country'.	*Titus Andronicus* *Henry VI, Parts I, II and III* *Richard III*
1593	London theatres closed by the plague. Christopher Marlowe killed in a Deptford tavern.	*Two Gentlemen of Verona* *Comedy of Errors* *The Taming of the Shrew* *Love's Labour's Lost*
1594	Shakespeare's company becomes The Lord Chamberlain's Men.	*Romeo and Juliet*

1595	Raleigh's first expedition to Guiana. Last expedition of Drake and Hawkins (both died).	*Richard II* *A Midsummer Night's Dream*
1596	Spenser's *Faerie Queene* (Books IV–VI) published. James Burbage buys rooms at Blackfriars and begins to convert them into a theatre.	*King John* *The Merchant of Venice* Shakespeare's son Hamnet dies. Shakespeare's father is granted a coat of arms.
1597	James Burbage dies, his son Richard, a famous actor, turns the Blackfriars Theatre into a private playhouse.	*Henry IV (Part I)* Shakespeare buys and redecorates New Place at Stratford.
1598	Death of Philip II of Spain	*Henry IV (Part II)* *Much Ado About Nothing*
1599	Death of Edmund Spenser. The Globe Theatre completed at Bankside by Richard and Cuthbert Burbage.	*Henry V* *Julius Caesar* *As You Like It*
1600	Fortune Theatre built at Cripplegate. East India Company founded for the extension of English trade and influence in the East. The Children of the Chapel begin to use the hall at Blackfriars.	*Merry Wives of Windsor* *Troilus and Cressida*
1601		*Hamlet*
1602	Sir Thomas Bodley's library opened at Oxford.	*Twelfth Night*
1603	Death of Queen Elizabeth. James I comes to the throne. Shakespeare's company becomes The King's Men. Raleigh tried, condemned and sent to the Tower	
1604	Treaty of peace with Spain	*Measure for Measure* *Othello* *All's Well that Ends Well*
1605	The Gunpowder Plot: an attempt by a group of Catholics to blow up the Houses of Parliament.	

1606	Guy Fawkes and other plotters executed.	*Macbeth* *King Lear*
1607	Virginia, in America, colonized. A great frost in England.	*Antony and Cleopatra* *Timon of Athens* *Coriolanus* Shakespeare's daughter, Susanna, married to Dr. John Hall.
1608	The company of the Children of the Chapel Royal (who had performed at Blackfriars for ten years) is disbanded. John Milton born. Notorious pirates executed in London.	Richard Burbage leases the Blackfriars Theatre to six of his fellow actors, including Shakespeare. *Pericles, Prince of Tyre*
1609		Shakespeare's Sonnets published.
1610	A great drought in England	*Cymbeline*
1611	Chapman completes his great translation of the *Iliad*, the story of Troy. Authorized Version of the Bible published.	*A Winter's Tale* *The Tempest*
1612	Webster's *The White Devil* first staged.	Shakespeare's brother, Gilbert, dies.
1613	Globe theatre burnt down during a performance of *Henry VIII* (the firing of small cannon set fire to the thatched roof). Webster's *Duchess of Malfi* first staged.	*Henry VIII* *Two Noble Kinsmen* Shakespeare buys a house at Blackfriars.
1614	Globe Theatre rebuilt in 'far finer manner than before'.	
1616	Ben Jonson publishes his plays in one volume. Raleigh released from the Tower in order to prepare an expedition to the gold mines of Guiana.	Shakespeare's daughter, Judith, marries Thomas Quiney. Death of Shakespeare on his birthday, April 23rd.
1618	Raleigh returns to England and is executed on the charge for which he was imprisoned in 1603.	
1623	Publication of the Folio edition of Shakespeare's plays	Death of Anne Shakespeare (née Hathaway).

Life & Times

William Shakespeare the Playwright

There exists a curious paradox when it comes to the life of William Shakespeare. He easily has more words written about him than any other famous English writer, yet we know the least about him. This inevitably means that most of what is written about him is either fabrication or speculation. The reason why so little is known about Shakespeare is that he wasn't a novelist or a historian or a man of letters. He was a playwright, and playwrights were considered fairly low on the social pecking order in Elizabethan society. Writing plays was about providing entertainment for the masses – the great unwashed. It was the equivalent to being a journalist for a tabloid newspaper.

In fact, we only know of Shakespeare's work because two of his friends had the foresight to collect his plays together following his death and have them printed. The only reason they did so was apparently because they rated his talent and thought it would be a shame if his words were lost.

Consequently his body of work has ever since been assessed and reassessed as the greatest contribution to English literature. That is despite the fact that we know that different printers took it upon themselves to heavily edit the material they worked from. We also know that Elizabethan plays were worked and reworked frequently, so that they evolved over time until they were honed to perfection, which means that many different hands played their part in the active writing process. It would therefore be fair to say that any play attributed to Shakespeare is unlikely to contain a great deal of original input. Even the plots were based on well known historical events, so it would be hard to know what fragments of any Shakespeare play came from that single mind.

One might draw a comparison with the Christian bible, which remains such a compelling read because it came from the collaboration of many contributors and translators over centuries, who each adjusted the stories until they could no longer be improved. As virtually nothing is known of Shakespeare's life and even less about his method of working, we shall never know the truth about his plays. They certainly contain some very elegant phrasing, clever plot devices and plenty of words never before seen in print, but as to whether Shakespeare invented them from a unique imagination or whether he simply took them from others around him is anyone's guess.

The best bet seems to be that Shakespeare probably took the lead role in devising the original drafts of the plays, but was open to collaboration from any source when it came to developing them into workable scripts for effective performances. He would have had to work closely with his fellow actors in rehearsals, thereby finding out where to edit, abridge, alter, reword and so on.

In turn, similar adjustments would have occurred in his absence, so that definitive versions of his plays never really existed. In effect Shakespeare was only responsible for providing the framework of plays, upon which others took liberties over time. This wasn't helped by the fact that the English language itself was not definitive at that time either. The consequence was that people took it upon themselves to spell words however they pleased or to completely change words and phrasing to suit their own preferences.

It is easy to see then, that Shakespeare's plays were always going to have lives of their own, mutating and distorting in detail like Chinese whispers. The culture of creative preservation was simply not established in Elizabethan England. Creative ownership of Shakespeare's plays was lost to him as soon as he released them into the consciousness of others. They saw nothing wrong with taking his ideas and running with them, because no one had ever suggested that one shouldn't, and Shakespeare probably regarded his work in the same way. His plays weren't sacrosanct works of art, they were templates for theatre folk to make their livings from, so they had every right to mould them into productions that drew in the crowds as effectively as possible. Shakespeare was like the helmsman of a sailing ship, steering the vessel but wholly reliant on the team work of his crew to arrive at the desired destination.

It seems that Shakespeare certainly had a natural gift, but the genius of his plays may be attributable to the collective efforts of Shakespeare and others. It is a rather satisfying notion to think that *his* plays might actually be the creative outpourings of the Elizabethan milieu in which Shakespeare immersed himself. That makes them important social documents as well as seminal works of the English language.

Money in Shakespeare's Day

It is extremely difficult, if not impossible, to relate the value of money in our time to its value in another age and to compare prices of commodities today and in the past. Many items *are* simply not comparable on grounds of quality or serviceability.

There was a bewildering variety of coins in use in Elizabethan England. As nearly all English and European coins were gold or silver, they had intrinsic value apart from their official value. This meant that foreign coins circulated freely in England and were officially recognized, for example the French crown (écu) worth about 30p (72 cents), and the Spanish ducat worth about 33p (79 cents). The following table shows some of the coins mentioned by Shakespeare and their relation to one another.

GOLD	British	American	SILVER	British	American
sovereign (heavy type)	£1.50	$3.60	shilling	10p	24c
sovereign (light type)	66p–£1	$1.58–$2.40	groat	1.5p	4c
angel					
royal	33p–50p	79c–$1.20			
noble	50p	$1.20			
crown	25p	60c			

A comparison of the following prices in Shakespeare's time with the prices of the same items today will give some idea of the change in the value of money.

ITEM	PRICE British	American	ITEM	PRICE British	American
beef, per lb.	0.5p	1c	cherries (lb.)	1p	2c
mutton, leg	7.5p	18c	7 oranges	1p	2c
rabbit	3.5p	9c	1 lemon	1p	2c
chicken	3p	8c	cream (quart)	2.5p	6c
potatoes (lb)	10p	24c	sugar (lb.)	£1	$2.40
carrots (bunch)	1p	2c	sack (wine) (gallon)	14p	34c
8 artichokes	4p	9c	tobacco (oz.)	25p	60c
1 cucumber	1p	2c	biscuits (lb.)	12.5p	30c

INTRODUCTION

As a budding playwright, Shakespeare was attacked by an older writer, Robert Greene, for plagiarism: 'an upstart Crow, beautified with our feathers'. Towards the end of his career, for his next-to-last play to be completed, Shakespeare drew upon a story by this same Greene, and so created *The Winter's Tale*.

In Shakespeare's own period, older playgoers, remembering Greene and seeing this work for the first time, must have thought they knew how it ended. The king, consumed by jealousy, repudiates his queen, who dies. He soon after recognises his error, but it is too late. That, at least, is the story of Greene's *Pandosto*. Shakespeare, however, picks up this simple tale and turns it into a myth of resurrection. We all, like the early playgoers, think Hermione to be dead. We see her fall, deadly sick, on stage. News of her death is brought by Paulina, whom we know to be a reliable witness. Sixteen years pass, without any sign of her.

Tragedy lies very close to comedy here. The earlier episodes, the autumn and winter parts of the play, display the imagery of disease and dearth: 'Why then the world and all that's in't is nothing;/The covering sky is nothing; Bohemia nothing;/my wife is nothing; nor nothing have those nothings,/If this be nothing'. But those corrugated rhythms give way to the comedy of Autolycus and his song of spring: 'When daffodils begin to peer,/With heigh! the doxy over the dale'. There is the daughter who was thought lost, Perdita in her harvest scene, also evoking the spring: 'daffodils,/That come before the swallow dares, and take/The winds of March with beauty'. This prefigures the restoration of Hermione, which is the key to the play.

The meeting of Perdita with Leontes, her father, which could have been one of Shakespeare's reconciliation set-pieces, is reported at second hand in order to preserve the grand climax for the restitution of Hermione. There, at the end, is the Statue Scene when Hermione rises, as though from the dead, and joins her repentant husband.

So far from attempting to seem naturalistic, the text drives home the impossibilities: 'That she is living,/Were it but told you, should be hooted at/Like an old tale'. But Shakespeare has paid the 'old tale' of his former enemy, Robert Greene, the supreme compliment of turning it into high drama. Leontes says, 'I saw her,/As I thought, dead; and have, in vain, said many/A prayer upon her grave'. However, the prayers have not been in vain. The whole scene is an acting out of resurrection.

The extravagance of the plot is matched by that of the structure. Such critics as the Italian, Castelvetro, and the Englishman, Sir Philip Sidney, thought that the Greek philosopher, Aristotle, had imposed rules on the drama that decreed restrictions as to the time a play should encompass in its action, the place – only one – it should represent, and the plot – very simple – that it should deploy. These rules were called 'unities', and Shakespeare violated these unities in an exuberant fashion. The action covers sixteen years, and not smoothly: there is a gaping void between Act 3 and Act 4. The scenes swerve between Sicily, the kingdom of Leontes, and Bohemia, the kingdom of his supposed rival, Polixenes. The plot, as we have seen, is far-fetched beyond all decorum. However, the appeal is not to the intricacies of art, but to nature. In the end, what we are shown is nature's own cycle, represented in the death and restoration of Hermione. She is a kind of earth goddess. We see the earth die, every winter. Yet it revives in the spring. It is an idea similar to that of Jesus' parable of the Prodigal Son. He 'was dead, and is alive again; he was lost, and is found' (Luke 15:24).

LIST OF CHARACTERS

Leontes	King of Sicilia
Mamillius	his son, the young Prince of Sicilia
Camillo *Antigonus* *Cleomenes* *Dion*	} lords of Sicilia
Polixenes	King of Bohemia
Florizel	his son, Prince of Bohemia
Archidamus	a lord of Bohemia
Old Shepherd	reputed father of Perdita
Clown	his son
Autolycus	a rogue
A Mariner A Gaoler	
Time	as Chorus
Hermione	Queen to Leontes
Perdita	daughter to Leontes and Hermione
Paulina	wife to Antigonus
Emilia	a lady attending on the Queen
Mopsa *Dorcas*	} shepherdesses

Other Lords, Gentlemen, Ladies, Officers, Servants,
Shepherds, and Shepherdesses

The scene: Sicilia And Bohemia.

ACT ONE
Scene I

Sicilia. The palace of Leontes.

[Enter CAMILLO and ARCHIDAMUS.]

Archidamus
If you shall chance, Camillo, to visit Bohemia, on the like occasion whereon my services are now on foot, you shall see, as I have said, great difference betwixt our Bohemia and your Sicilia.

Camillo
I think this coming summer the King of Sicilia means to 5
pay Bohemia the visitation which he justly owes him.

Archidamus
Wherein our entertainment shall shame us we will be justified in our loves; for indeed –

Camillo
Beseech you –

Archidamus
Verily, I speak it in the freedom of my knowledge: we 10
cannot with such magnificence, in so rare – I know not what to say. We will give you sleepy drinks, that your senses, unintelligent of our insufficience, may, though they cannot praise us, as little accuse us.

Camillo
You pay a great deal too dear for what's given freely. 15

Archidamus
Believe me, I speak as my understanding instructs me and as mine honesty puts it to utterance.

Camillo
Sicilia cannot show himself over-kind to Bohemia. They were train'd together in their childhoods; and there rooted betwixt them then such an affection 20
which cannot choose but branch now. Since their more

mature dignities and royal necessities made separation of their society, their encounters, though not personal, have been royally attorneyed with interchange of gifts,
25 letters, loving embassies; that they have seem'd to be together, though absent; shook hands, as over a vast; and embrac'd as it were from the ends of opposed winds. The heavens continue their loves!

Archidamus

I think there is not in the world either malice or
30 matter to alter it. You have an unspeakable comfort of your young Prince Mamillius; it is a gentleman of the greatest promise that ever came into my note.

Camillo

I very well agree with you in the hopes of him. It is a gallant child; one that indeed physics the subject,
35 makes old hearts fresh; they that went on crutches ere he was born desire yet their life to see him a man.

Archidamus

Would they else be content to die?

Camillo

Yes; if there were no other excuse why they should desire to live.

Archidamus

40 If the King had no son, they would desire to live on crutches till he had one.

[Exeunt.]

Scene II

Sicilia. The palace of Leontes.

[Enter LEONTES, POLIXENES, HERMIONE, MAMILLIUS, CAMILLO, and Attendants.]

Polixenes
    Nine changes of the wat'ry star hath been
    The shepherd's note since we have left our throne
    Without a burden. Time as long again
    Would be fill'd up, my brother, with our thanks;
    And yet we should for perpetuity   5
    Go hence in debt. And therefore, like a cipher,
    Yet standing in rich place, I multiply
    With one 'We thank you' many thousands moe
    That go before it.

Leontes
               Stay your thanks a while,
    And pay them when you part.

Polixenes
                    Sir, that's to-morrow.   10
    I am question'd by my fears of what may chance
    Or breed upon our absence, that may blow
    No sneaping winds at home, to make us say
    'This is put forth too truly'. Besides, I have stay'd
    To tire your royalty.

Leontes
               We are tougher, brother,   15
    Than you can put us to't.

Polixenes
               No longer stay.

Leontes
    One sev'night longer.

Polixenes
               Very sooth, to-morrow.

Leontes
    We'll part the time between's then; and in that

    I'll no gainsaying.
Polixenes

                  Press me not, beseech you, so.
    There is no tongue that moves, none, none i' th'
20   world,
    So soon as yours could win me. So it should now,
    Were there necessity in your request, although
    'Twere needful I denied it. My affairs
    Do even drag me homeward; which to hinder
25   Were in your love a whip to me; my stay
    To you a charge and trouble. To save both,
    Farewell, our brother.
Leontes

               Tongue-tied, our Queen? Speak you.
Hermione
    I had thought, sir, to have held my peace until
    You had drawn oaths from him not to stay. You, sir,
30   Charge him too coldly. Tell him you are sure
    All in Bohemia's well – this satisfaction
    The by-gone day proclaim'd. Say this to him,
    He's beat from his best ward.
Leontes

                    Well said, Hermione.
Hermione
    To tell he longs to see his son were strong;
35   But let him say so then, and let him go;
    But let him swear so, and he shall not stay;
    We'll thwack him hence with distaffs.
    [To POLIXENES*]* Yet of your royal presence I'll
      adventure
    The borrow of a week. When at Bohemia
40   You take my lord, I'll give him my commission
    To let him there a month behind the gest
    Prefix'd for's parting. – Yet, good deed, Leontes,
    I love thee not a jar o' th' clock behind
    What lady she her lord. – You'll stay?

Polixenes

No, madam.

Hermione

Nay, but you will?

Polixenes

I may not, verily. 45

Hermione

Verily!
You put me off with limber vows; but I,
Though you would seek t' unsphere the stars with
    oaths,
Should yet say 'Sir, no going'. Verily,
You shall not go; a lady's 'verily' is
As potent as a lord's. Will you go yet? 50
Force me to keep you as a prisoner,
Not like a guest; so you shall pay your fees
When you depart, and save your thanks. How say
    you?
My prisoner or my guest? By your dread 'verily',
One of them you shall be.

Polixenes

Your guest, then, madam: 55
To be your prisoner should import offending;
Which is for me less easy to commit
Than you to punish.

Hermione

Not your gaoler then,
But your kind hostess. Come, I'll question you
Of my lord's tricks and yours when you were boys. 60
You were pretty lordings then!

Polixenes

We were, fair Queen,
Two lads that thought there was no more behind
But such a day to-morrow as to-day,
And to be boy eternal.

Hermione

Was not my lord

65   The verier wag o' th' two?

Polixenes

We were as twinn'd lambs that did frisk i' th' sun
And bleat the one at th' other. What we chang'd
Was innocence for innocence; we knew not
The doctrine of ill-doing, nor dream'd
70   That any did. Had we pursu'd that life,
And our weak spirits ne'er been higher rear'd
With stronger blood, we should have answer'd heaven
Boldly 'Not guilty', the imposition clear'd
Hereditary ours.

Hermione

              By this we gather
You have tripp'd since.

Polixenes

75   O my most sacred lady,
Temptations have since then been born to 's, for
In those unfledg'd days was my wife a girl;
Your precious self had then not cross'd the eyes
Of my young playfellow.

Hermione

                 Grace to boot!
80   Of this make no conclusion, lest you say
Your queen and I are devils. Yet, go on;
Th' offences we have made you do we'll answer,
If you first sinn'd with us, and that with us
You did continue fault, and that you slipp'd not
With any but with us.

Leontes

85   Is he won yet?

Hermione

He'll stay, my lord.

Leontes

             At my request he would not.
Hermione, my dearest, thou never spok'st
To better purpose.

Hermione
                    Never?
Leontes
                              Never but once.
Hermione
    What! Have I twice said well? When was't before?
    I prithee tell me; cram's with praise, and make's   90
    As fat as tame things. One good deed dying tongueless
    Slaughters a thousand waiting upon that.
    Our praises are our wages; you may ride's
    With one soft kiss a thousand furlongs ere
    With spur we heat an acre. But to th' goal: 95
    My last good deed was to entreat his stay;
    What was my first? It has an elder sister,
    Or I mistake you. O, would her name were Grace!
    But once before I spoke to th' purpose – When?
    Nay, let me have't; I long.   100
Leontes
    Why, that was when
    Three crabbed months had sour'd themselves to
        death,
    Ere I could make thee open thy white hand
    And clap thyself my love; then didst thou utter
    'I am yours for ever'.
Hermione
                    'Tis Grace indeed.   105
    Why, lo you now, I have spoke to th' purpose twice:
    The one for ever earn'd a royal husband;
    Th' other for some while a friend.

                    [Giving her hand to POLIXENES.*]*

Leontes
    [Aside]   Too hot, too hot!
    To mingle friendship far is mingling bloods.
    I have tremor cordis on me; my heart dances,   110
    But not for joy, not joy. This entertainment
    May a free face put on; derive a liberty

From heartiness, from bounty, fertile bosom,
And well become the agent. 'T may, I grant;

115 But to be paddling palms and pinching fingers,
As now they are, and making practis'd smiles
As in a looking-glass; and then to sigh, as 'twere
The mort o' th' deer. O, that is entertainment
My bosom likes not, nor my brows! Mamillius,
Art thou my boy?

Mamillius

Ay, my good lord.

Leontes

120 I' fecks!
Why, that's my bawcock. What! hast smutch'd thy
    nose?
They say it is a copy out of mine. Come, Captain,
We must be neat – not neat, but cleanly, Captain.
And yet the steer, the heifer, and the calf,

125 Are all call'd neat. – Still virginalling
Upon his palm? – How now, you wanton calf,
Art thou my calf?

Mamillius

Yes, if you will, my lord.

Leontes

Thou want'st a rough pash and the shoots that I have,
To be full like me; yet they say we are

130 Almost as like as eggs. Women say so,
That will say any thing. But were they false
As o'er-dy'd blacks, as wind, as waters – false
As dice are to be wish'd by one that fixes
No bourn 'twixt his and mine; yet were it true

135 To say this boy were like me. Come, sir page,
Look on me with your welkin eye. Sweet villain!
Most dear'st! my collop! Can thy dam? – may't be?
Affection! thy intention stabs the centre.
Thou dost make possible things not so held,

140 Communicat'st with dreams – how can this be? –
With what's unreal thou coactive art,

And fellow'st nothing. Then 'tis very credent
Thou mayst co-join with something; and thou dost –
And that beyond commission; and I find it,
And that to the infection of my brains   145
And hard'ning of my brows.

Polixenes

                    What means Sicilia?

Hermione

    He something seems unsettled.

Polixenes

                      How, my lord!
What cheer? How is't with you, best brother?

Hermione

                      You look
As if you held a brow of much distraction.
Are you mov'd, my lord?

Leontes

                No, in good earnest.   150
How sometimes nature will betray its folly,
Its tenderness, and make itself a pastime
To harder bosoms! Looking on the lines
Of my boy's face, me thoughts I did recoil
Twenty-three years; and saw myself unbreech'd,   155
In my green velvet coat; my dagger muzzl'd,
Lest it should bite its master and so prove,
As ornaments oft do, too dangerous.
How like, methought, I then was to this kernel,
This squash, this gentleman. Mine honest friend,   160
Will you take eggs for money?

Mamillius

    No, my lord, I'll fight.

Leontes

    You will? Why, happy man be's dole! My brother,
Are you so fond of your young prince as we
Do seem to be of ours?

Polixenes

165   If at home, sir,
He's all my exercise, my mirth, my matter;
Now my sworn friend, and then mine enemy;
My parasite, my soldier, statesman, all.
He makes a July's day short as December,
170 And with his varying childness cures in me
Thoughts that would thick my blood.

Leontes

                               So stands this squire
Offic'd with me. We two will walk, my lord,
And leave you to your graver steps. Hermione,
How thou lov'st us show in our brother's welcome;
175 Let what is dear in Sicily be cheap;
Next to thyself and my young rover, he's
Apparent to my heart.

Hermione

                       If you would seek us,
We are yours i' th' garden. Shall's attend you there?

Leontes

To your own bents dispose you; you'll be found,
180 Be you beneath the sky. *[Aside]* I am angling now,
Though you perceive me not how I give line.
Go to, go to!
How she holds up the neb, the bill to him!
And arms her with the boldness of a wife
To her allowing husband!

       [Exeunt POLIXENES, HERMIONE, *and Attendants.]*

185   Gone already!
Inch-thick, knee-deep, o'er head and ears a fork'd one!
Go, play, boy, play; thy mother plays, and I
Play too; but so disgrac'd a part, whose issue
Will hiss me to my grave. Contempt and clamour
190 Will be my knell. Go, play, boy, play. There have been,
Or I am much deceiv'd, cuckolds ere now;
And many a man there is, even at this present,

Now while I speak this, holds his wife by th' arm
That little thinks she has been sluic'd in's absence,
And his pond fish'd by his next neighbour, by   195
Sir Smile, his neighbour. Nay, there's comfort in't,
Whiles other men have gates and those gates open'd,
As mine, against their will. Should all despair
That have revolted wives, the tenth of mankind
Would hang themselves. Physic for't there's none;   200
It is a bawdy planet, that will strike
Where 'tis predominant; and 'tis pow'rful, think it,
From east, west, north, and south. Be it concluded,
No barricado for a belly. Know't,
It will let in and out the enemy   205
With bag and baggage. Many thousand on's
Have the disease, and feel't not. How now, boy!

Mamillius

I am like you, they say.

Leontes

                 Why, that's some comfort.
What! Camillo there?

Camillo

Ay, my good lord.   210

Leontes

Go play, Mamillius; thou'rt an honest man.
   [Exit MAMILLIUS.]
Camillo, this great sir will yet stay longer.

Camillo

You had much ado to make his anchor hold;
When you cast out, it still came home.

Leontes

                 Didst note it?

Camillo

He would not stay at your petitions; made   215
His business more material.

Leontes

                 Didst perceive it?
[Aside] They're here with me already; whisp'ring,
   rounding,

'Sicilia is a so-forth'. 'Tis far gone
When I shall gust it last. – How came't, Camillo,
That he did stay?

Camillo

220   At the good Queen's entreaty.

Leontes

'At the Queen's' be't. 'Good' should be pertinent;
But so it is, it is not. Was this taken
By any understanding pate but thine?
For thy conceit is soaking, will draw in

225 More than the common blocks. Not noted, is't,
But of the finer natures, by some severals
Of head-piece extraordinary? Lower messes
Perchance are to this business purblind? Say.

Camillo

Business, my lord? I think most understand
Bohemia stays here longer.

Leontes

                          Ha?

Camillo

230   Stays here longer.

Leontes

Ay, but why?

Camillo

To satisfy your Highness, and the entreaties
Of our most gracious mistress.

Leontes

                          Satisfy

Th' entreaties of your mistress! Satisfy!

235 Let that suffice. I have trusted thee, Camillo,
With all the nearest things to my heart, as well
My chamber-councils, wherein, priest-like, thou
Hast cleans'd my bosom – I from thee departed
Thy penitent reform'd; but we have been

240 Deceiv'd in thy integrity, deceiv'd
In that which seems so.

Camillo
                    Be it forbid, my lord!
Leontes
    To bide upon't: thou art not honest; or,
    If thou inclin'st that way, thou art a coward,
    Which hoxes honesty behind, restraining
    From course requir'd; or else thou must be counted   245
    A servant grafted in my serious trust,
    And therein negligent; or else a fool
    That seest a game play'd home, the rich stake drawn,
    And tak'st it all for jest.
Camillo
                    My gracious lord,
    I may be negligent, foolish, and fearful: 250
    In every one of these no man is free
    But that his negligence, his folly, fear,
    Among the infinite doings of the world,
    Sometime puts forth. In your affairs, my lord,
    If ever I were wilful-negligent,   255
    It was my folly; if industriously
    I play'd the fool, it was my negligence,
    Not weighing well the end; if ever fearful
    To do a thing where I the issue doubted,
    Whereof the execution did cry out   260
    Against the non-performance, 'twas a fear
    Which oft infects the wisest. These, my lord,
    Are such allow'd infirmities that honesty
    Is never free of. But, beseech your Grace,
    Be plainer with me; let me know my trespass   265
    By its own visage; if I then deny it,
    'Tis none of mine.
Leontes
                    Ha' not you seen, Camillo –
    But that's past doubt; you have, or your eye-glass
    Is thicker than a cuckold's horn – or heard –
    For to a vision so apparent rumour   270
    Cannot be mute – or thought – for cogitation

Resides not in that man that does not think –
My wife is slippery? If thou wilt confess –
Or else be impudently negative,
275 To have nor eyes nor ears nor thought – then say
My wife's a hobby-horse, deserves a name
As rank as any flax-wench that puts to
Before her troth-plight. Say't and justify't.

Camillo

I would not be a stander-by to hear
280 My sovereign mistress clouded so, without
My present vengeance taken. Shrew my heart!
You never spoke what did become you less
Than this; which to reiterate were sin
As deep as that, though true.

Leontes

                                  Is whispering nothing?
285 Is leaning cheek to cheek? Is meeting noses?
Kissing with inside lip? Stopping the career
Of laughter with a sigh? – a note infallible
Of breaking honesty. Horsing foot on foot?
Skulking in corners? Wishing clocks more swift;
290 Hours, minutes; noon, midnight? And all eyes
Blind with the pin and web but theirs, theirs only,
That would unseen be wicked – is this nothing?
Why, then the world and all that's in't is nothing;
The covering sky is nothing; Bohemia nothing;
295 My wife is nothing; nor nothing have these nothings,
If this be nothing.

Camillo

                   Good my lord, be cur'd
Of this diseas'd opinion, and betimes;
For 'tis most dangerous.

Leontes

                 Say it be, 'tis true.

Camillo

No, no, my lord.

Leontes

            It is; you lie, you lie.
I say thou liest, Camillo, and I hate thee;   300
Pronounce thee a gross lout, a mindless slave,
Or else a hovering temporizer that
Canst with thine eyes at once see good and evil,
Inclining to them both. Were my wife's liver
Infected as her life, she would not live   305
The running of one glass.

Camillo

              Who does infect her?

Leontes

Why, he that wears her like her medal, hanging
About his neck, Bohemia; who – if I
Had servants true about me that bare eyes
To see alike mine honour as their profits,   310
Their own particular thrifts, they would do that
Which should undo more doing. Ay, and thou,
His cupbearer – whom I from meaner form
Have bench'd and rear'd to worship; who mayst see,
Plainly as heaven sees earth and earth sees heaven,   315
How I am gall'd – mightst bespice a cup
To give mine enemy a lasting wink;
Which draught to me were cordial.

Camillo

                 Sir, my lord,
I could do this; and that with no rash potion,
But with a ling'ring dram that should not work   320
Maliciously like poison. But I cannot
Believe this crack to be in my dread mistress,
So sovereignly being honourable.
I have lov'd thee –

Leontes

        Make that thy question, and go rot!
Dost think I am so muddy, so unsettled,   325
To appoint myself in this vexation; sully
The purity and whiteness of my sheets –

Which to preserve is sleep, which being spotted
Is goads, thorns, nettles, tails of wasps;
330 Give scandal to the blood o' th' Prince, my son –
Who I do think is mine, and love as mine –
Without ripe moving to 't? Would I do this?
Could man so blench?

Camillo

I must believe you, sir.
I do; and will fetch off Bohemia for't;
335 Provided that, when he's remov'd, your Highness
Will take again your queen as yours at first,
Even for your son's sake; and thereby for sealing
The injury of tongues in courts and kingdoms
Known and allied to yours.

Leontes

Thou dost advise me
340 Even so as I mine own course have set down.
I'll give no blemish to her honour, none.

Camillo

My lord,
Go then; and with a countenance as clear
As friendship wears at feasts, keep with Bohemia
345 And with your queen. I am his cupbearer;
If from me he have wholesome beverage,
Account me not your servant.

Leontes

This is all:
Do't, and thou hast the one half of my heart;
Do't not, thou split'st thine own.

Camillo

I'll do't, my lord.

Leontes

350 I will seem friendly, as thou hast advis'd me.   *[Exit.]*

Camillo

O miserable lady! But, for me,
What case stand I in? I must be the poisoner
Of good Polixenes; and my ground to do't

Is the obedience to a master; one
Who, in rebellion with himself, will have   355
All that are his so too. To do this deed,
Promotion follows. If I could find example
Of thousands that had struck anointed kings
And flourish'd after, I'd not do't; but since
Nor brass, nor stone, nor parchment, bears not one,   360
Let villainy itself forswear't. I must
Forsake the court. To do't, or no, is certain
To me a break-neck. Happy star reign now!
Here comes Bohemia.

[Enter POLIXENES.]

Polixenes

            This is strange. Methinks
My favour here begins to warp. Not speak?   365
Good day, Camillo.
Camillo

          Hail, most royal sir!
Polixenes

What is the news i' th' court?
Camillo

               None rare, my lord.
Polixenes

The King hath on him such a countenance
As he had lost some province, and a region
Lov'd as he loves himself; even now I met him   370
With customary compliment, when he,
Wafting his eyes to th' contrary and falling
A lip of much contempt, speeds from me; and
So leaves me to consider what is breeding
That changes thus his manners.   375
Camillo

I dare not know, my lord.
Polixenes

How, dare not! Do not. Do you know, and dare not
Be intelligent to me? 'Tis thereabouts;

For, to yourself, what you do know, you must,
380 And cannot say you dare not. Good Camillo,
Your chang'd complexions are to me a mirror
Which shows me mine chang'd too; for I must be
A party in this alteration, finding
Myself thus alter'd with't.

Camillo

There is a sickness
385 Which puts some of us in distemper; but
I cannot name the disease; and it is caught
Of you that yet are well.

Polixenes

How! caught of me?
Make me not sighted like the basilisk;
I have look'd on thousands who have sped the better
390 By my regard, but kill'd none so. Camillo –
As you are certainly a gentleman; thereto
Clerk-like experienc'd, which no less adorns
Our gentry than our parents' noble names,
In whose success we are gentle – I beseech you,
395 If you know aught which does behove my knowledge
Thereof to be inform'd, imprison't not
In ignorant concealment.

Camillo

I may not answer.

Polixenes

A sickness caught of me, and yet I well?
I must be answer'd. Dost thou hear, Camillo?
400 I conjure thee, by all the parts of man
Which honour does acknowledge, whereof the least
Is not this suit of mine, that thou declare
What incidency thou dost guess of harm
Is creeping toward me; how far off, how near;
405 Which way to be prevented, if to be;
If not, how best to bear it.

Camillo
                              Sir, I will tell you;
Since I am charg'd in honour, and by him
That I think honourable. Therefore mark my counsel,
Which must be ev'n as swiftly followed as
I mean to utter it, or both yourself and me   410
Cry lost, and so goodnight.

Polixenes
                              On, good Camillo.

Camillo
I am appointed him to murder you.

Polixenes
By whom, Camillo?

Camillo
                              By the King.

Polixenes
                              For what?

Camillo
He thinks, nay, with all confidence he swears,
As he had seen 't or been an instrument   415
To vice you to't, that you have touch'd his queen
Forbiddenly.

Polixenes
                    O, then my best blood turn
To an infected jelly, and my name
Be yok'd with his that did betray the Best!
Turn then my freshest reputation to   420
A savour that may strike the dullest nostril
Where I arrive, and my approach be shunn'd,
Nay, hated too, worse than the great'st infection
That e'er was heard or read!

Camillo
                              Swear his thought over
By each particular star in heaven and   425
By all their influences, you may as well
Forbid the sea for to obey the moon
As or by oath remove or counsel shake

23

The fabric of his folly, whose foundation
430   Is pil'd upon his faith and will continue
The standing of his body.

Polixenes
                           How should this grow?

Camillo
I know not; but I am sure 'tis safer to
Avoid what's grown than question how 'tis born.
If therefore you dare trust my honesty,
435   That lies enclosed in this trunk which you
Shall bear along impawn'd, away to-night.
Your followers I will whisper to the business;
And will, by twos and threes, at several posterns,
Clear them o' th' city. For myself, I'll put
440   My fortunes to your service, which are here
By this discovery lost. Be not uncertain,
For, by the honour of my parents, I
Have utt'red truth; which if you seek to prove,
I dare not stand by; nor shall you be safer
Than one condemn'd by the King's own mouth,
445   thereon
His execution sworn.

Polixenes
                           I do believe thee:
I saw his heart in's face. Give me thy hand;
Be pilot to me, and thy places shall
Still neighbour mine. My ships are ready, and
450   My people did expect my hence departure
Two days ago. This jealousy
Is for a precious creature; as she's rare,
Must it be great; and, as his person's mighty,
Must it be violent; and as he does conceive
455   He is dishonour'd by a man which ever
Profess'd to him, why, his revenges must
In that be made more bitter. Fear o'er-shades me.
Good expedition be my friend, and comfort
The gracious Queen, part of his theme, but nothing

Of his ill-ta'en suspicion! Come, Camillo;   460
I will respect thee as a father, if
Thou bear'st my life off hence. Let us avoid.
Camillo
It is in mine authority to command
The keys of all the posterns. Please your Highness
To take the urgent hour. Come, sir, away.   465

[Exeunt.]

ACT TWO
Scene I

Sicilia. The palace of Leontes.

[Enter HERMIONE, MAMILLIUS, and Ladies.]

Hermione
Take the boy to you; he so troubles me,
'Tis past enduring.

1 Lady
                              Come, my gracious lord,
Shall I be your playfellow?

Mamillius
                                              No, I'll none of you.

1 Lady
Why, my sweet lord?

Mamillius
5   You'll kiss me hard, and speak to me as if
I were a baby still. I love you better.

2 Lady
And why so, my lord?

Mamillius
                              Not for because
Your brows are blacker; yet black brows, they say,
Become some women best; so that there be not
10   Too much hair there, but in a semicircle
Or a half-moon made with a pen.

2 Lady
                                              Who taught't this?

Mamillius
I learn'd it out of women's faces. Pray now,
What colour are your eyebrows?

1 Lady
                                              Blue, my lord.

Mamillius
>Nay, that's a mock. I have seen a lady's nose
>That has been blue, but not her eyebrows.

1 Lady
>   Hark ye: 15
>The Queen your mother rounds apace. We shall
>Present our services to a fine new prince
>One of these days; and then you'd wanton with us,
>If we would have you.

2 Lady
>   She is spread of late
>Into a goodly bulk. Good time encounter her! 20

Hermione
>What wisdom stirs amongst you? Come, sir, now
>I am for you again. Pray you sit by us,
>And tell's a tale.

Mamillius
>   Merry or sad shall't be?

Hermione
>As merry as you will.

Mamillius
>A sad tale's best for winter. I have one 25
>Of sprites and goblins.

Hermione
>   Let's have that, good sir.
>Come on, sit down; come on, and do your best
>To fright me with your sprites; you're pow'rful at it.

Mamillius
>There was a man –

Hermione
>   Nay, come, sit down; then on.

Mamillius
>Dwelt by a churchyard – I will tell it softly; 30
>Yond crickets shall not hear it.

Hermione
>   Come on then,
>And give't me in mine ear.

[Enter LEONTES, ANTIGONUS, Lords and Others.]

Leontes
　　Was he met there? his train? Camillo with him?
1 Lord
　　Behind the tuft of pines I met them; never
35　Saw I men scour so on their way. I ey'd them
　　Even to their ships.
Leontes
　　　　　　　　How blest am I
　　In my just censure, in my true opinion!
　　Alack, for lesser knowledge! How accurs'd
　　In being so blest! There may be in the cup
40　A spider steep'd, and one may drink, depart,
　　And yet partake no venom, for his knowledge
　　Is not infected; but if one present
　　Th' abhorr'd ingredient to his eye, make known
　　How he hath drunk, he cracks his gorge, his sides,
45　With violent hefts. I have drunk, and seen the spider.
　　Camillo was his help in this, his pander.
　　There is a plot against my life, my crown;
　　All's true that is mistrusted. That false villain
　　Whom I employ'd was pre-employ'd by him;
50　He has discover'd my design, and I
　　Remain a pinch'd thing; yea, a very trick
　　For them to play at will. How came the posterns
　　So easily open?
1 Lord
　　　　　　　　By his great authority;
　　Which often hath no less prevail'd than so
　　On your command.
Leontes
55　　　　　　　　I know't too well.
　　Give me the boy. I am glad you did not nurse him;
　　Though he does bear some signs of me, yet you
　　Have too much blood in him.
Hermione
　　　　　　　　　　What is this? Sport?

Leontes

Bear the boy hence; he shall not come about her;
Away with him; and let her sport herself   60

                       [MAMILLIUS is led out.]

With that she's big with – for 'tis Polixenes
Has made thee swell thus.

Hermione

                    But I'd say he had not,
And I'll be sworn you would believe my saying,
Howe'er you lean to th' nayward.

Leontes

                      You, my lords,
Look on her, mark her well; be but about   65
To say 'She is a goodly lady' and
The justice of your hearts will thereto add
'Tis pity she's not honest – honourable'.
Praise her but for this her without-door form,
Which on my faith deserves high speech, and straight   70
The shrug, the hum or ha, these petty brands
That calumny doth use – O, I am out! –
That mercy does, for calumny will sear
Virtue itself – these shrugs, these hum's and ha's,
When you have said she's goodly, come between,   75
Ere you can say she's honest. But be't known,
From him that has most cause to grieve it should be,
She's an adultress.

Hermione

                Should a villain say so,
The most replenish'd villain in the world,
He were as much more villain: you, my lord,   80
Do but mistake.

Leontes

             You have mistook, my lady,
Polixenes for Leontes. O thou thing!
Which I'll not call a creature of thy place,
Lest barbarism, making me the precedent,
Should a like language use to all degrees   85

And mannerly distinguishment leave out
Betwixt the prince and beggar. I have said
She's an adulteress; I have said with whom.
More, she's a traitor; and Camillo is
90   A federary with her, and one that knows
What she should shame to know herself
But with her most vile principal – that she's
A bed-swerver, even as bad as those
That vulgars give bold'st titles; ay, and privy
To this their late escape.

Hermione
95   No, by my life,
Privy to none of this. How will this grieve you,
When you shall come to clearer knowledge, that
You thus have publish'd me! Gentle my lord,
You scarce can right me throughly then to say
You did mistake.

Leontes
100   No; if I mistake
In those foundations which I build upon,
The centre is not big enough to bear
A school-boy's top. Away with her to prison.
He who shall speak for her is afar off guilty
But that he speaks.

Hermione
105   There's some ill planet reigns.
I must be patient till the heavens look
With an aspect more favourable. Good my lords,
I am not prone to weeping, as our sex
Commonly are – the want of which vain dew
110   Perchance shall dry your pities – but I have
That honourable grief lodg'd here which burns
Worse than tears drown. Beseech you all, my lords,
With thoughts so qualified as your charities
Shall best instruct you, measure me; and so
The King's will be perform'd!

Leontes

    [To the Guard]   Shall I be heard?   115

Hermione

    Who is't that goes with me? Beseech your Highness
    My women may be with me, for you see
    My plight requires it. Do not weep, good fools;
    There is no cause; when you shall know your mistress
    Has deserv'd prison, then abound in tears   120
    As I come out: this action I now go on
    Is for my better grace. Adieu, my lord.
    I never wish'd to see you sorry; now
    I trust I shall. My women, come; you have leave.

Leontes

    Go, do our bidding; hence!   125

    [Exeunt HERMIONE, *guarded, and ladies.]*

Lord

    Beseech your Highness, call the Queen again.

Antigonus

    Be certain what you do, sir, lest your justice
    Prove violence, in the which three great ones suffer,
    Yourself, your queen, your son.

1 Lord

                      For her, my lord,
    I dare my life lay down – and will do't, sir,   130
    Please you t' accept it – that the Queen is spotless
    I' th' eyes of heaven and to you – I mean
    In this which you accuse her.

Antigonus

                      If it prove
    She's otherwise, I'll keep my stables where
    I lodge my wife; I'll go in couples with her;   135
    Than when I feel and see her no farther trust her;
    For every inch of woman in the world,
    Ay, every dram of woman's flesh is false,
    If she be.

Leontes

        Hold your peaces.

1 Lord

             Good my lord –

Antigonus

140   It is for you we speak, not for ourselves.
      You are abus'd, and by some putter-on
      That will be damn'd for't. Would I knew the villain!
      I would land-damn him. Be she honour-flaw'd –
      I have three daughters: the eldest is eleven;
145   The second and the third, nine and some five;
      If this prove true, they'll pay for't. By mine honour,
      I'll geld 'em all; fourteen they shall not see
      To bring false generations. They are co-heirs;
      And I had rather glib myself than they
      Should not produce fair issue.

Leontes

150   Cease; no more.
      You smell this business with a sense as cold
      As is a dead man's nose; but I do see't and feel't
      As you feel doing thus; and see withal
      The instruments that feel.

Antigonus

                     If it be so,
155   We need no grave to bury honesty;
      There's not a grain of it the face to sweeten
      Of the whole dungy earth.

Leontes

                What! Lack I credit?

1 Lord

      I had rather you did lack than I, my lord,
      Upon this ground; and more it would content me
160   To have her honour true than your suspicion,
      Be blam'd for't how you might.

Leontes

                   Why, what need we
      Commune with you of this, but rather follow

Our forceful instigation? Our prerogative
Calls not your counsels; but our natural goodness
Imparts this; which, if you – or stupified   165
Or seeming so in skill – cannot or will not
Relish a truth like us, inform yourselves
We need no more of your advice. The matter,
The loss, the gain, the ord'ring on't, is all
Properly ours.

Antigonus
                              And I wish, my liege,   170
You had only in your silent judgment tried it,
Without more overture.

Leontes
                              How could that be?
Either thou art most ignorant by age,
Or thou wert born a fool. Camillo's flight,
Added to their familiarity –   175
Which was as gross as ever touch'd conjecture,
That lack'd sight only, nought for approbation
But only seeing, all other circumstances
Made up to th' deed – doth push on this proceeding.
Yet, for a greater confirmation –   180
For, in an act of this importance, 'twere
Most piteous to be wild – I have dispatch'd in post
To sacred Delphos, to Apollo's temple,
Cleomenes and Dion, whom you know
Of stuff'd sufficiency. Now, from the oracle   185
They will bring all, whose spiritual counsel had,
Shall stop or spur me. Have I done well?

I Lord
Well done, my lord.

Leontes
Though I am satisfied, and need no more
Than what I know, yet shall the oracle   190
Give rest to th' minds of others such as he
Whose ignorant credulity will not
Come up to th' truth. So have we thought it good

From our free person she should be confin'd,
195 Lest that the treachery of the two fled hence
Be left her to perform. Come, follow us;
We are to speak in public; for this business
Will raise us all.

Antigonus
[Aside] To laughter, as I take it,
100 If the good truth were known.

[Exeunt.]

Scene II

Sicilia. A prison.

[Enter PAULINA, *a Gentleman, and Attendants.]*

Paulina

> The keeper of the prison – call to him;
> Let him have knowledge who I am.   *[Exit Gentleman.]*
>   Good lady!
>
> No court in Europe is too good for thee;
> What dost thou then in prison?

> *[Re-enter Gentleman with the Gaoler.]*

> Now, good sir,   5
> You know me, do you not?

Gaoler

>   For a worthy lady,
> And one who much I honour.

Paulina

>   Pray you, then,
> Conduct me to the Queen.

Gaoler

>   I may not, madam;
> To the contrary I have express commandment.

Paulina

> Here's ado, to lock up honesty and honour from   10
> Th' access of gentle visitors! Is't lawful, pray you,
> To see her women – any of them? Emilia?

Gaoler

> So please you, madam,
> To put apart these your attendants, I
> Shall bring Emilia forth.

Paulina

>   I pray now, call her.   15
> Withdraw yourselves.   *[Exeunt Attendants.]*

Gaoler

>   And, madam,
> I must be present at your conference.

Paulina

> Well, be't so, prithee.   *[Exit Gaoler.]*
> Here's such ado to make no stain a stain
> As passes colouring.

>   *[Re-enter Gaoler, with* EMILIA.*]*

20   Dear gentlewoman,
> How fares our gracious lady?

Emilia

> As well as one so great and so forlorn
> May hold together. On her frights and griefs,
> Which never tender lady hath borne greater,
25 She is, something before her time, deliver'd.

Paulina

> A boy?

Emilia

>   A daughter, and a goodly babe,
> Lusty, and like to live. The Queen receives
> Much comfort in't; says 'My poor prisoner,
> I am as innocent as you'.

Paulina

>   I dare be sworn.
> These dangerous unsafe lunes i' th' King, beshrew
30   them!
> He must be told on't, and he shall. The office
> Becomes a woman best; I'll take't upon me;
> If I prove honey-mouth'd, let my tongue blister,
> And never to my red-look'd anger be
35 The trumpet any more. Pray you, Emilia,
> Commend my best obedience to the Queen;
> If she dares trust me with her little babe,
> I'll show't the King, and undertake to be
> Her advocate to th' loud'st. We do not know
40 How he may soften at the sight o' th' child:
> The silence often of pure innocence

Persuades when speaking fails.
Emilia

                        Most worthy madam,
Your honour and your goodness is so evident
That your free undertaking cannot miss
A thriving issue; there is no lady living   45
So meet for this great errand. Please your ladyship
To visit the next room, I'll presently
Acquaint the Queen of your most noble offer;
Who but to-day hammer'd of this design,
But durst not tempt a minister of honour,   50
Lest she should be denied.
Paulina

                  Tell her, Emilia,
I'll use that tongue I have; if wit flow from't
As boldness from my bosom, let't not be doubted
I shall do good.
Emilia

             Now be you blest for it!
I'll to the Queen. Please you come something nearer. 55
Gaoler

Madam, if't please the Queen to send the babe,
I know not what I shall incur to pass it,
Having no warrant.
Paulina

             You need not fear it, sir.
This child was prisoner to the womb, and is
By law and process of great Nature thence   60
Freed and enfranchis'd – not a party to
The anger of the King, nor guilty of,
If any be, the trespass of the Queen.
Gaoler

I do believe it.
Paulina

Do not you fear. Upon mine honour, I   65
Will stand betwixt you and danger.

[Exeunt.]

Scene III

Sicilia. The palace of Leontes.

[Enter LEONTES, ANTIGONUS, Lords, and Servants.]

Leontes
    Nor night nor day no rest! It is but weakness
    To bear the matter thus – mere weakness. If
    The cause were not in being – part o' th' cause,
    She, th' adultress; for the harlot king
5   Is quite beyond mine arm, out of the blank
    And level of my brain, plot-proof; but she
    I can hook to me – say that she were gone,
    Given to the fire, a moiety of my rest
    Might come to me again. Who's there?

1 Servant
                          My lord?

Leontes
    How does the boy?

1 Servant
10   He took good rest to-night;
    'Tis hop'd his sickness is discharg'd.

Leontes
    To see his nobleness!
    Conceiving the dishonour of his mother,
    He straight declin'd, droop'd, took it deeply,
15   Fasten'd and fix'd the shame on't in himself,
    Threw off his spirit, his appetite, his sleep,
    And downright languish'd. Leave me solely. Go,
    See how he fares. *[Exit Servant]* Fie, fie! no thought of
        him!
    The very thought of my revenges that way
20   Recoil upon me – in himself too mighty,
    And in his parties, his alliance. Let him be,
    Until a time may serve; for present vengeance,
    Take it on her. Camillo and Polixenes
    Laugh at me, make their pastime at my sorrow.

They should not laugh if I could reach them; nor   25
Shall she, within my pow'r.

[Enter PAULINA, with a Child.]

1 Lord
                              You must not enter.
Paulina
   Nay, rather, good my lords, be second to me.
   Fear you his tyrannous passion more, alas,
   Than the Queen's life? A gracious innocent soul,
   More free than he is jealous.
Antigonus
                              That's enough.   30
2 Servant
   Madam, he hath not slept tonight; commanded
   None should come at him.
Paulina
                              Not so hot, good sir;
   I come to bring him sleep. 'Tis such as you,
   That creep like shadows by him, and do sigh
   At each his needless heavings – such as you   35
   Nourish the cause of his awaking: I
   Do come with words as medicinal as true,
   Honest as either, to purge him of that humour
   That presses him from sleep.
Leontes
                              What noise there, ho?
Paulina
   No noise, my lord; but needful conference   40
   About some gossips for your Highness.
Leontes
                              How!
   Away with that audacious lady! Antigonus,
   I charg'd thee that she should not come about me;
   I knew she would.
Antigonus
                     I told her so, my lord,

45 On your displeasure's peril, and on mine,
    She should not visit you.

Leontes

                        What, canst not rule her?

Paulina

    From all dishonesty he can: in this,
    Unless he take the course that you have done –
    Commit me for committing honour – trust it,
    He shall not rule me.

Antigonus

50   La you now, you hear!
    When she will take the rein, I let her run;
    But she'll not stumble.

Paulina

                        Good my liege, I come –
    And I beseech you hear me, who professes
    Myself your loyal servant, your physician,
55 Your most obedient counsellor; yet that dares
    Less appear so, in comforting your evils,
    Than such as most seem yours – I say I come
    From your good Queen.

Leontes

                    Good Queen!

Paulina

    Good Queen, my lord, good Queen – I say good
        Queen;
60 And would by combat make her good, so were I
    A man, the worst about you.

Leontes

                        Force her hence.

Paulina

    Let him that makes but trifles of his eyes.
    First hand me. On mine own accord I'll off;
    But first I'll do my errand. The good Queen,
65 For she is good, hath brought you forth a daughter;
    Here 'tis; commends it to your blessing.

                              [Laying down the child.]

Leontes

Out!

A mankind witch! Hence with her, out o' door!
A most intelligencing bawd!

Paulina

Not so.

I am as ignorant in that as you
In so entitling me; and no less honest   70
Than you are mad; which is enough, I'll warrant,
As this world goes, to pass for honest.

Leontes

Traitors!

Will you not push her out? Give her the bastard.
[To ANTIGONUS*]* Thou dotard, thou art woman-tir'd,
     unroosted
By thy Dame Partlet here. Take up the bastard;   75
Take't up, I say; give't to thy crone.

Paulina

For ever

Unvenerable be thy hands, if thou
Tak'st up the Princess by that forced baseness
Which he has put upon't!

Leontes

He dreads his wife.

Paulina

So I would you did; then 'twere past all doubt   80
You'd call your children yours.

Leontes

A nest of traitors!

Antigonus

I am none, by this good light.

Paulina

Nor I; nor any

But one that's here; and that's himself; for he
The sacred honour of himself, his Queen's,
His hopeful son's, his babe's, betrays to slander,   85
Whose sting is sharper than the sword's; and will not –

For, as the case now stands, it is a curse
He cannot be compell'd to 't – once remove
The root of his opinion, which is rotten
As ever oak or stone was sound.

Leontes

90   A callat
Of boundless tongue, who late hath beat her husband,
And now baits me! This brat is none of mine;
It is the issue of Polixenes.
Hence with it, and together with the dam
Commit them to the fire.

Paulina

95   It is yours.
And, might we lay th' old proverb to your charge,
So like you 'tis the worse. Behold, my lords,
Although the print be little, the whole matter
And copy of the father – eye, nose, lip,

100   The trick of's frown, his forehead; nay, the valley,
The pretty dimples of his chin and cheek; his smiles;
The very mould and frame of hand, nail, finger.
And thou, good goddess Nature, which hast made it
So like to him that got it, if thou hast

105   The ordering of the mind too, 'mongst all colours
No yellow in't, lest she suspect, as he does,
Her children not her husband's!

Leontes

                                      A gross hag!
And, lozel, thou art worthy to be hang'd
That wilt not stay her tongue.

Antigonus

                                Hang all the husbands

110   That cannot do that feat, you'll leave yourself
Hardly one subject.

Leontes

                          Once more, take her hence.

Paulina

A most unworthy and unnatural lord
Can do no more.

Leontes
                         I'll ha' thee burnt.
Paulina
                                   I care not.
It is an heretic that makes the fire,
Not she which burns in't. I'll not call you tyrant;   115
But this most cruel usage of your Queen –
Not able to produce more accusation
Than your own weak-hing'd fancy – something
    savours
Of tyranny, and will ignoble make you,
Yea, scandalous to the world.
Leontes
                         On your allegiance,   120
Out of the chamber with her! Were I a tyrant,
Where were her life? She durst not call me so,
If she did know me one. Away with her!
Paulina
I pray you, do not push me; I'll be gone.
Look to your babe, my lord; 'tis yours. Jove send her   125
A better guiding spirit! What needs these hands?
You that are thus so tender o'er his follies
Will never do him good, not one of you.
So, so. Farewell; we are gone.   *[Exit.]*
Leontes
Thou, traitor, hast set on thy wife to this.   130
My child! Away with't. Even thou, that hast
A heart so tender o'er it, take it hence,
And see it instantly consum'd with fire;
Even thou, and none but thou. Take it up straight.
Within this hour bring me word 'tis done,   135
And by good testimony, or I'll seize thy life,
With what thou else call'st thine. If thou refuse,
And wilt encounter with my wrath, say so;
The bastard brains with these my proper hands
Shall I dash out. Go, take it to the fire;   140
For thou set'st on thy wife.

Antigonus

I did not, sir.
These lords, my noble fellows, if they please,
Can clear me in't.

Lords

We can. My royal liege,
He is not guilty of her coming hither.

Leontes

145   You're liars all.

1 Lord

Beseech your Highness, give us better credit.
We have always truly serv'd you; and beseech
So to esteem of us; and on our knees we beg,
As recompense of our dear services
150   Past and to come, that you do change this purpose,
Which being so horrible, so bloody, must
Lead on to some foul issue. We all kneel.

Leontes

I am a feather for each wind that blows.
Shall I live on to see this bastard kneel
155   And call me father? Better burn it now
Than curse it then. But be it; let it live.
It shall not neither. *[To* ANTIGONUS*]* You, sir, come
    you hither.
You that have been so tenderly officious
With Lady Margery, your midwife there,
160   To save this bastard's life – for 'tis a bastard,
So sure as this beard's grey – what will you adventure
To save this brat's life?

Antigonus

Anything, my lord,
That my ability may undergo,
And nobleness impose. At least, thus much:
165   I'll pawn the little blood which I have left
To save the innocent – anything possible.

Leontes

It shall be possible. Swear by this sword
Thou wilt perform my bidding.

Antigonus

        I will, my lord.

Leontes

 Mark, and perform it – seest thou? For the fail
 Of any point in't shall not only be   170
 Death to thyself, but to thy lewd-tongu'd wife,
 Whom for this time we pardon. We enjoin thee,
 As thou art liegeman to us, that thou carry
 This female bastard hence; and that thou bear it
 To some remote and desert place, quite out   175
 Of our dominions; and that there thou leave it,
 Without more mercy, to it own protection
 And favour of the climate. As by strange fortune
 It came to us, I do in justice charge thee,
 On thy soul's peril and thy body's torture,   180
 That thou commend it strangely to some place
 Where chance may nurse or end it. Take it up.

Antigonus

 I swear to do this, though a present death
 Had been more merciful. Come on, poor babe.
 Some powerful spirit instruct the kites and ravens 185
 To be thy nurses! Wolves and bears, they say,
 Casting their savageness aside, have done
 Like offices of pity. Sir, be prosperous
 In more than this deed does require! And blessing
 Against this cruelty fight on thy side,   190
 Poor thing, condemn'd to loss!

        [Exit with the child.]

Leontes

      No, I'll not rear
 Another's issue.

    [Enter a Servant.]

Servant

     Please your Highness, posts
 From those you sent to th' oracle are come
 An hour since. Cleomenes and Dion,

195 Being well arriv'd from Delphos, are both landed,
Hasting to th' court.

1 Lord

So please you, sir, their speed
Hath been beyond account.

Leontes

Twenty-three days
They have been absent; 'tis good speed; foretells
The great Apollo suddenly will have
200 The truth of this appear. Prepare you, lords;
Summon a session, that we may arraign
Our most disloyal lady; for, as she hath
Been publicly accus'd, so shall she have
A just and open trial. While she lives,
205 My heart will be a burden to me. Leave me;
And think upon my bidding.

[Exeunt.]

ACT THREE
Scene I

Sicilia. On the road to the Capital.

[Enter CLEOMENES *and* DION.*]*

Cleomenes
    The climate's delicate, the air most sweet,
    Fertile the isle, the temple much surpassing
    The common praise it bears.
Dion
                     I shall report,
    For most it caught me, the celestial habits –
    Methinks I so should term them – and the reverence   5
    Of the grave wearers. O, the sacrifice!
    How ceremonious, solemn, and unearthly,
    It was i' th' off'ring!
Cleomenes
               But of all, the burst
    And the ear-deaf'ning voice o' th' oracle,
    Kin to Jove's thunder, so surpris'd my sense   10
    That I was nothing.
Dion
            If th' event o' th' journey
    Prove as successful to the Queen – O, be't so! –
    As it hath been to us rare, pleasant, speedy,
    The time is worth the use on't.
Cleomenes
              Great Apollo
    Turn all to th' best! These proclamations,   15
    So forcing faults upon Hermione,
    I little like.
Dion
         The violent carriage of it
    Will clear or end the business. When the oracle –

Thus by Apollo's great divine seal'd up –
20 Shall the contents discover, something rare
Even then will rush to knowledge. Go; fresh horses.
And gracious be the issue!

[Exeunt.]

Scene II

Sicilia. A court of justice.

Enter LEONTES, *Lords, and Officers.]*

Leontes

This sessions, to our great grief we pronounce,
Even pushes 'gainst our heart – the party tried,
The daughter of a king, our wife, and one
Of us too much belov'd. Let us be clear'd
Of being tyrannous, since we so openly   5
Proceed in justice, which shall have due course,
Even to the guilt or the purgation.
Produce the prisoner.

Officer

It is his Highness' pleasure that the Queen
Appear in person here in court.

[Enter HERMIONE, *as to her trial,* PAULINA, *and Ladies.]*

Silence!   10

Leontes

Read the indictment.

Officer

[Reads] 'Hermione, Queen to the worthy Leontes,
King of Sicilia, thou art here accused and arraigned of
high treason, in committing adultery with Polixenes,
King of Bohemia; and conspiring with Camillo to take   15
away the life of our sovereign lord the King, thy royal
husband: the pretence whereof being by circumstances
partly laid open, thou, Hermione, contrary to the faith
and allegiance of a true subject, didst counsel and aid
them, for their better safety, to fly away by night.'   20

Hermione

Since what I am to say must be but that
Which contradicts my accusation, and
The testimony on my part no other
But what comes from myself, it shall scarce boot me

25　To say 'Not guilty'. Mine integrity
　　Being counted falsehood shall, as I express it,
　　Be so receiv'd. But thus – if pow'rs divine
　　Behold our human actions, as they do,
　　I doubt not then but innocence shall make
30　False accusation blush, and tyranny
　　Tremble at patience. You, my lord, best know –
　　Who least will seem to do so – my past life
　　Hath been as continent, as chaste, as true,
　　As I am now unhappy; which is more
35　Than history can pattern, though devis'd
　　And play'd to take spectators; for behold me –
　　A fellow of the royal bed, which owe
　　A moiety of the throne, a great king's daughter,
　　The mother to a hopeful prince – here standing
40　To prate and talk for life and honour fore
　　Who please to come and hear. For life, I prize it
　　As I weigh grief, which I would spare; for honour,
　　'Tis a derivative from me to mine,
　　And only that I stand for. I appeal
45　To your own conscience, sir, before Polixenes
　　Came to your court, how I was in your grace,
　　How merited to be so; since he came,
　　With what encounter so uncurrent I
　　Have strain'd t' appear thus; if one jot beyond
50　The bound of honour, or in act or will
　　That way inclining, hard'ned be the hearts
　　Of all that hear me, and my near'st of kin
　　Cry fie upon my grave!

Leontes

　　　　　　　　　I ne'er heard yet
　　That any of these bolder vices wanted
55　Less impudence to gainsay what they did
　　Than to perform it first.

Hermione

　　　　　　　　　That's true enough;
　　Though 'tis a saying, sir, not due to me.

Leontes

You will not own it.

Hermione

                  More than mistress of
Which comes to me in name of fault, I must not
At all acknowledge. For Polixenes,   60
With whom I am accus'd, I do confess
I lov'd him as in honour he requir'd;
With such a kind of love as might become
A lady like me; with a love even such,
So and no other, as yourself commanded;   65
Which not to have done, I think had been in me
Both disobedience and ingratitude
To you and toward your friend; whose love had spoke,
Even since it could speak, from an infant, freely,
That it was yours. Now for conspiracy: 70
I know not how it tastes, though it be dish'd
For me to try how; all I know of it
Is that Camillo was an honest man;
And why he left your court, the gods themselves,
Wotting no more than I, are ignorant.   75

Leontes

You knew of his departure, as you know
What you have underta'en to do in's absence.

Hermione

Sir,
You speak a language that I understand not.
My life stands in the level of your dreams,   80
Which I'll lay down.

Leontes

                  Your actions are my dreams.
You had a bastard by Polixenes,
And I but dream'd it. As you were past all shame –
Those of your fact are so – so past all truth;
Which to deny concerns more than avails; for as   85
Thy brat hath been cast out, like to itself,
No father owning it – which is indeed

More criminal in thee than it – so thou
Shalt feel our justice; in whose easiest passage
Look for no less than death.

Hermione

90   Sir, spare your threats.
The bug which you would fright me with I seek.
To me can life be no commodity.
The crown and comfort of my life, your favour,
I do give lost, for I do feel it gone.

95   But know not how it went; my second joy
And first fruits of my body, from his presence
I am barr'd, like one infectious; my third comfort,
Starr'd most unluckily, is from my breast –
The innocent milk in it most innocent mouth –

100   Hal'd out to murder; myself on every post
Proclaim'd a strumpet; with immodest hatred
The child-bed privilege denied, which 'longs
To women of all fashion; lastly, hurried
Here to this place, i' th' open air, before

105   I have got strength of limit. Now, my liege,
Tell me what blessings I have here alive
That I should fear to die. Therefore proceed.
But yet hear this – mistake me not: no life,
I prize it not a straw, but for mine honour

110   Which I would free – if I shall be condemn'd
Upon surmises, all proofs sleeping else
But what your jealousies awake, I tell you
'Tis rigour, and not law. Your honours all,
I do refer me to the oracle:
Apollo be my judge!

Lord

115   This your request
Is altogether just. Therefore, bring forth,
And in Apollo's name, his oracle.

[Exeunt certain Officers.]

Hermione
The Emperor of Russia was my father;

O that he were alive, and here beholding
His daughter's trial! that he did but see   120
The flatness of my misery; yet with eyes
Of pity, not revenge!

    [Re-enter Officers, with CLEOMENES *and* DION.]

Officer
You here shall swear upon this sword of justice
That you, Cleomenes and Dion, have
Been both at Delphos, and from thence have brought   125
This seal'd-up oracle, by the hand deliver'd
Of great Apollo's priest; and that since then
You have not dar'd to break the holy seal
Nor read the secrets in't.

Cleomenes, Dion
                 All this we swear.

Leontes
Break up the seals and read.   130

Officer
[Reads] 'Hermione is chaste; Polixenes blameless;
Camillo a true subject; Leontes a jealous tyrant; his
innocent babe truly begotten; and the King shall live
without an heir, if that which is lost be not found.'

Lords
Now blessed be the great Apollo!

Hermione
                 Praised!   135

Leontes
Hast thou read truth?

Officer
              Ay, my lord; even so
As it is here set down.

Leontes
There is no truth at all i' th' oracle.
The sessions shall proceed. This is mere falsehood.

    [Enter a Servant.]

Servant
    My lord the King, the King!

Leontes

140   What is the business?

Servant
    O sir, I shall be hated to report it:
    The Prince your son, with mere conceit and fear
    Of the Queen's speed, is gone.

Leontes

                       How! Gone?

Servant

                              Is dead.

Leontes
    Apollo's angry; and the heavens themselves
    Do strike at my injustice   *[HERMIONE swoons.]*

145   How now, there!

Paulina
    This news is mortal to the Queen. Look down
    And see what death is doing.

Leontes

                    Take her hence.
    Her heart is but o'ercharg'd; she will recover.
    I have too much believ'd mine own suspicion.

150   Beseech you tenderly apply to her
    Some remedies for life.

       [Exeunt PAULINA and Ladies with HERMIONE.]

                  Apollo, pardon
    My great profaneness 'gainst thine oracle.
    I'll reconcile me to Polixenes,
    New woo my queen, recall the good Camillo –

155   Whom I proclaim a man of truth, of mercy.
    For, being transported by my jealousies
    To bloody thoughts and to revenge, I chose
    Camillo for the minister to poison
    My friend Polixenes; which had been done

160   But that the good mind of Camillo tardied

My swift command, though I with death and with
Reward did threaten and encourage him,
Not doing it and being done. He, most humane
And fill'd with honour, to my kingly guest
Unclasp'd my practice, quit his fortunes here,   165
Which you knew great, and to the certain hazard
Of all incertainties himself commended,
No richer than his honour. How he glisters
Thorough my rust! And how his piety
Does my deeds make the blacker!

[Re-enter PAULINA.]

Paulina

                          Woe the while!   170
O, cut my lace, lest my heart, cracking it,
Break too!

1 Lord

           What fit is this, good lady?

Paulina

What studied torments, tyrant, hast for me?
What wheels, racks, fires? what flaying, boiling
In leads or oils? What old or newer torture   175
Must I receive, whose every word deserves
To taste of thy most worst? Thy tyranny
Together working with thy jealousies,
Fancies too weak for boys, too green and idle
For girls of nine – O, think what they have done,   180
And then run mad indeed, stark mad; for all
Thy by-gone fooleries were but spices of it.
That thou betray'dst Polixenes, 'twas nothing;
That did but show thee, of a fool, inconstant,
And damnable ingrateful. Nor was't much   185
Thou wouldst have poison'd good Camillo's honour,
To have him kill a king – poor trespasses,
More monstrous standing by; whereof I reckon
The casting forth to crows thy baby daughter
To be or none or little, though a devil   190

Would have shed water out of fire ere done't;
Nor is't directly laid to thee, the death
Of the young Prince, whose honourable thoughts –
Thoughts high for one so tender – cleft the heart
195 That could conceive a gross and foolish sire
Blemish'd his gracious dam. This is not, no,
Laid to thy answer; but the last – O lords,
When I have said, cry 'Woe!' – the Queen, the Queen,
The sweet'st, dear'st creature's dead; and vengeance
for't
Not dropp'd down yet.

Lord
200   The higher pow'rs forbid!

Paulina
I say she's dead; I'll swear't. If word nor oath
Prevail not, go and see. If you can bring
Tincture or lustre in her lip, her eye,
Heat outwardly or breath within, I'll serve you
205 As I would do the gods. But, O thou tyrant!
Do not repent these things, for they are heavier
Than all thy woes can stir; therefore betake thee
To nothing but despair. A thousand knees
Ten thousand years together, naked, fasting,
210 Upon a barren mountain, and still winter
In storm perpetual, could not move the gods
To look that way thou wert.

Leontes
                              Go on, go on.
Thou canst not speak too much; I have deserv'd
All tongues to talk their bitt'rest.

1 Lord
                              Say no more;
215 Howe'er the business goes, you have made fault
I' th' boldness of your speech.

Paulina
                              I am sorry for't.
All faults I make, when I shall come to know them,

I do repent. Alas, I have show'd too much
The rashness of a woman! He is touch'd
To th' noble heart. What's gone and what's past help 220
Should be past grief. Do not receive affliction
At my petition; I beseech you, rather
Let me be punish'd that have minded you
Of what you should forget. Now, good my liege,
Sir, royal sir, forgive a foolish woman. 225
The love I bore your queen – lo, fool again!
I'll speak of her no more, nor of your children;
I'll not remember you of my own lord,
Who is lost too. Take your patience to you,
And I'll say nothing.

Leontes

     Thou didst speak but well 230
When most the truth; which I receive much better
Than to be pitied of thee. Prithee, bring me
To the dead bodies of my queen and son.
One grave shall be for both. Upon them shall
The causes of their death appear, unto 235
Our shame perpetual. Once a day I'll visit
The chapel where they lie; and tears shed there
Shall be my recreation. So long as nature
Will bear up with this exercise, so long
I daily vow to use it. Come, and lead me 240
To these sorrows.

[Exeunt.]

Scene III

Bohemia. The sea-coast.

[Enter ANTIGONUS *with the Child, and a Mariner].*

Antigonus
    Thou art perfect then our ship hath touch'd upon
    The deserts of Bohemia?
Mariner
                       Ay, my lord, and fear
    We have landed in ill time; the skies look grimly
    And threaten present blusters. In my conscience,
5   The heavens with that we have in hand are angry
    And frown upon's.
Antigonus
    Their sacred wills be done! Go, get aboard;
    Look to thy bark. I'll not be long before
    I call upon thee.
Mariner
10   Make your best haste; and go not
    Too far i' th' land; 'tis like to be loud weather;
    Besides, this place is famous for the creatures
    Of prey that keep upon't.
Antigonus
                  Go thou away;
    I'll follow instantly.
Mariner
               I am glad at heart
    To be so rid o' th' business.   *[Exit.]*
Antigonus
15   Come, poor babe.
    I have heard, but not believ'd, the spirits o' th' dead
    May walk again. If such thing be, thy mother
    Appear'd to me last night; for ne'er was dream
    So like a waking. To me comes a creature,
20   Sometimes her head on one side some another –
    I never saw a vessel of like sorrow,

So fill'd and so becoming; in pure white robes,
Like very sanctity, she did approach
My cabin where I lay; thrice bow'd before me;
And, gasping to begin some speech, her eyes   25
Became two spouts; the fury spent, anon
Did this break from her: 'Good Antigonus,
Since fate, against thy better disposition,
Hath made thy person for the thrower-out
Of my poor babe, according to thine oath,   30
Places remote enough are in Bohemia,
There weep, and leave it crying; and, for the babe
Is counted lost for ever, Perdita
I prithee call't. For this ungentle business,
Put on thee by my lord, thou ne'er shalt see   35
Thy wife Paulina more'. And so, with shrieks,
She melted into air. Affrighted much,
I did in time collect myself, and thought
This was so and no slumber. Dreams are toys;
Yet, for this once, yea, superstitiously,   40
I will be squar'd by this. I do believe
Hermione hath suffer'd death, and that
Apollo would, this being indeed the issue
Of King Polixenes, it should here be laid,
Either for life or death, upon the earth   45
Of its right father. Blossom, speed thee well!
                              [Laying down the child.]
There lie, and there thy character; there these
                              [Laying down a bundle.]
Which may, if fortune please, both breed thee, pretty,
And still rest thine. The storm begins. Poor wretch,
That for thy mother's fault art thus expos'd   50
To loss and what may follow! Weep I cannot,
But my heart bleeds; and most accurs'd am I
To be by oath enjoin'd to this. Farewell!
The day frowns more and more. Thou'rt like to have
A lullaby too rough; I never saw   55
The heavens so dim by day.   *[Noise of hunt within]*

A savage clamour!
Well may I get aboard! This is the chase;
I am gone for ever.   *[Exit, pursued by a bear.]*

[Enter an OLD SHEPHERD.]

Shepherd

I would there were no age between ten and three and
60   twenty, or that youth would sleep out the rest; for
there is nothing in the between but getting wenches
with child, wronging the ancientry, stealing, fighting –
[Horns] Hark you now! Would any but these boil'd brains
of nineteen and two and twenty hunt this weather?
65   They have scar'd away two of my best sheep, which
I fear the wolf will sooner find than the master. If any
where I have them, 'tis by the sea-side, browsing of ivy.
Good luck, an't be thy will! What have we here? *[Taking
up the child]* Mercy on's, a barne! A very pretty barne. A
70   boy or a child, I wonder? A pretty one; a very pretty one
– sure, some scape. Though I am not bookish, yet I can
read waiting-gentle-woman in the scape. This has been
some stair-work, some trunk-work, some behind-door-
work; they were warmer that got this than the poor
75   thing is here. I'll take it up for pity; yet I'll tarry till my
son come; he halloo'd but even now. Whoa-ho-hoa!

[Enter CLOWN.]

Clown

Hilloa, loa!

Shepherd

What, art so near? If thou'lt see a thing to talk on when
thou art dead and rotten, come hither. What ail'st
80   thou, man?

Clown

I have seen two such sights, by sea and by land! But I
am not to say it is a sea, for it is now the sky; betwixt the
firmament and it you cannot thrust a bodkin's point.

Shepherd

Why, boy, how is it?

Clown

I would you did but see how it chafes, how it rages, 85
how it takes up the shore! But that's not to the point.
O, the most piteous cry of the poor souls! Sometimes
to see 'em, and not to see 'em; now the ship boring
the moon with her mainmast, and anon swallowed
with yeast and froth, as you'd thrust a cork into a hogs- 90
head. And then for the land service – to see how the
bear tore out his shoulder-bone; how he cried to me for
help, and said his name was Antigonus, a nobleman!
But to make an end of the ship – to see how the sea
flap-dragon'd it; but first, how the poor souls roared, 95
and the sea mock'd them; and how the poor gentleman
roared, and the bear mock'd him, both roaring louder
than the sea or weather.

Shepherd

Name of mercy, when was this, boy?

Clown

Now, now; I have not wink'd since I saw these sights; 100
the men are not yet cold under water, nor the bear half
din'd on the gentleman; he's at it now.

Shepherd

Would I had been by to have help'd the old man!

Clown

I would you had been by the ship-side, to have help'd
her; there your charity would have lack'd footing. 105

Shepherd

Heavy matters, heavy matters! But look thee here, boy.
Now bless thyself; thou met'st with things dying, I with
things new-born. Here's a sight for thee; look thee, a
bearing-cloth for a squire's child! Look thee here; take
up, take up, boy; open't. So, let's see – it was told me I 110
should be rich by the fairies. This is some changeling.
Open't. What's within, boy?

Clown

You're a made old man; if the sins of your youth are forgiven you, you're well to live. Gold! all gold!

Shepherd

115 This is fairy gold, boy, and 'twill prove so. Up with't, keep it close. Home, home, the next way! We are lucky, boy; and to be so still requires nothing but secrecy. Let my sheep go. Come, good boy, the next way home.

Clown

Go you the next way with your findings. I'll go see if
120 the bear be gone from the gentleman, and how much he hath eaten. They are never curst but when they are hungry. If there be any of him left, I'll bury it.

Shepherd

That's a good deed. If thou mayest discern by that which is left of him what he is, fetch me to th' sight
125 of him.

Clown

Marry, will I; and you shall help to put him i' th' ground.

Shepherd

'Tis a lucky day, boy; and we'll do good deeds on't.

[Exeunt.]

ACT FOUR
Scene I

[Enter TIME, the Chorus.]

Time

    I, that please some, try all, both joy and terror
    Of good and bad, that makes and unfolds error,
    Now take upon me, in the name of Time,
    To use my wings. Impute it not a crime
    To me or my swift passage that I slide   5
    O'er sixteen years, and leave the growth untried
    Of that wide gap, since it is in my pow'r
    To o'erthrow law, and in one self-born hour
    To plant and o'erwhelm custom. Let me pass
    The same I am, ere ancient'st order was   10
    Or what is now receiv'd. I witness to
    The times that brought them in; so shall I do
    To th' freshest things now reigning, and make stale
    The glistering of this present, as my tale
    Now seems to it. Your patience this allowing,   15
    I turn my glass, and give my scene such growing
    As you had slept between. Leontes leaving –
    Th' effects of his fond jealousies so grieving
    That he shuts up himself – imagine me,
    Gentle spectators, that I now may be   20
    In fair Bohemia; and remember well
    I mention'd a son o' th' King's, which Florizel
    I now name to you; and with speed so pace
    To speak of Perdita, now grown in grace
    Equal with wond'ring. What of her ensues   25
    I list not prophesy; but let Time's news
    Be known when 'tis brought forth. A shepherd's
        daughter,
    And what to her adheres, which follows after,
    Is th' argument of Time. Of this allow,

30   If ever you have spent time worse ere now;
If never, yet that Time himself doth say
He wishes earnestly you never may.

[Exit.]

Scene II

Bohemia. The palace of Polixenes.

[Enter POLIXENES *and* CAMILLO.]

Polixenes

I pray thee, good Camillo, be no more importunate: 'tis
a sickness denying thee anything; a death to grant this.

Camillo

It is fifteen years since I saw my country; though I have
for the most part been aired abroad, I desire to lay my
bones there. Besides, the penitent King, my master,   5
hath sent for me; to whose feeling sorrows I might be
some allay, or I o'erween to think so, which is another
spur to my departure.

Polixenes

As thou lov'st me, Camillo, wipe not out the rest of thy
services by leaving me now. The need I have of thee thine   10
own goodness hath made. Better not to have had thee
than thus to want thee; thou, having made me businesses
which none without thee can sufficiently manage, must
either stay to execute them thyself, or take away with
thee the very services thou hast done; which if I have not   15
enough considered – as too much I cannot – to be more
thankful to thee shall be my study; and my profit therein
the heaping friendships. Of that fatal country Sicilia,
prithee, speak no more; whose very naming punishes
me with the remembrance of that penitent, as thou   20
call'st him, and reconciled king, my brother; whose loss
of his most precious queen and children are even now
to be afresh lamented. Say to me, when saw'st thou
the Prince Florizel, my son? Kings are no less unhappy,
their issue not being gracious, than they are in losing   25
them when they have approved their virtues.

Camillo

Sir, it is three days since I saw the Prince. What his
happier affairs may be are to me unknown; but I have

30 missingly noted he is of late much retired from court, and is less frequent to his princely exercises than formerly he hath appeared.

Polixenes

I have considered so much, Camillo, and with some care, so far that I have eyes under my service which look upon his removedness; from whom I have this

35 intelligence, that he is seldom from the house of a most homely shepherd – a man, they say, that from very nothing, and beyond the imagination of his neighbours, is grown into an unspeakable estate.

Camillo

I have heard, sir, of such a man, who hath a daughter of

40 most rare note. The report of her is extended more than can be thought to begin from such a cottage.

Polixenes

That's likewise part of my intelligence; but, I fear, the angle that plucks our son thither. Thou shalt accompany us to the place; where we will, not appearing what we

45 are, have some question with the shepherd; from whose simplicity I think it not uneasy to get the cause of my son's resort thither. Prithee be my present partner in this business, and lay aside the thoughts of Sicilia.

Camillo

I willingly obey your command.

Polixenes

50 My best Camillo! We must disguise ourselves.

[Exeunt.]

Scene III

Bohemia. A road near the shepherd's cottage.

[Enter AUTOLYCUS, *singing.]*

When daffodils begin to peer,
   With heigh! the doxy over the dale,
Why, then comes in the sweet o' the year,
   For the red blood reigns in the winter's pale.
The white sheet bleaching on the hedge,   5
   With heigh! the sweet birds, O, how they sing!
Doth set my pugging tooth on edge,
   For a quart of ale is a dish for a king.
The lark, that tirra-lirra chants,
   With heigh! with heigh! the thrush and the jay,   10
Are summer songs for me and my aunts,
   While we lie tumbling in the hay.

I have serv'd Prince Florizel, and in my time
wore three-pile; but now I am out of service.

But shall I go mourn for that, my dear?   15
   The pale moon shines by night;
And when I wander here and there,
   I then do most go right.
If tinkers may have leave to live,
   And bear the sow-skin budget,   20
Then my account I well may give
   And in the stocks avouch it.

My traffic is sheets; when the kite builds, look to lesser
linen. My father nam'd me Autolycus; who, being, as I
am, litter'd under Mercury, was likewise a snapper-up of   25
unconsidered trifles. With die and drab I purchas'd this
caparison; and my revenue is the silly-cheat. Gallows
and knock are too powerful on the highway; beating

and hanging are terrors to me; for the life to come, I
30   sleep out the thought of it. A prize! a prize!

[Enter CLOWN.*]*

Clown

Let me see: every 'leven wether tods; every tod yields
pound and odd shilling; fifteen hundred shorn, what
comes the wool to?

Autolycus

[Aside] If the springe hold, the cock's mine.

Clown

35   I cannot do 't without counters. Let me see: what am
I to buy for our sheep-shearing feast? Three pound
of sugar, five pound of currants, rice – what will this
sister of mine do with rice? But my father hath made
her mistress of the feast, and she lays it on. She hath
40   made me four and twenty nosegays for the shearers –
three-man song-men all, and very good ones; but they
are most of them means and bases; but one Puritan
amongst them, and he sings psalms to hornpipes. I
must have saffron to colour the warden pies; mace;
45   dates – none, that's out of my note; nutmegs, seven; a
race or two of ginger, but that I may beg; four pound of
prunes, and as many of raisins o' th' sun.

Autolycus

[Grovelling on the ground] O that ever I was born!

Clown

I' th' name of me!

Autolycus

50   O, help me, help me! Pluck but off these rags; and then,
death, death!

Clown

Alack, poor soul! thou hast need of more rags to lay on
thee, rather than have these off.

Autolycus

O sir, the loathsomeness of them offend me more than
55   the stripes I have received, which are mighty ones and
millions.

Clown

Alas, poor man! a million of beating may come to a great matter.

Autolycus

I am robb'd, sir, and beaten; my money and apparel ta'en from me, and these detestable things put upon me. 60

Clown

What, by a horseman or a footman?

Autolycus

A footman, sweet sir, a footman.

Clown

Indeed, he should be a footman, by the garments he has left with thee; if this be a horseman's coat, it hath 65
seen very hot service. Lend me thy hand, I'll help thee. Come, lend me thy hand. *[Helping him up.]*

Autolycus

O, good sir, tenderly, O!

Clown

Alas, poor soul!

Autolycus

O, good sir, softly, good sir; I fear, sir, my shoulder 70
blade is out.

Clown

How now! Canst stand?

Autolycus

Softly, dear sir *[Picks his pocket]*; good sir, softly. You ha' done me a charitable office.

Clown

Dost lack any money? I have a little money for thee. 75

Autolycus

No, good sweet sir; no, I beseech you, sir. I have a kinsman not past three quarters of a mile hence, unto whom I was going; I shall there have money or anything I want. Offer me no money, I pray you; that kills my heart. 80

Clown

What manner of fellow was he that robb'd you?

Autolycus

A fellow, sir, that I have known to go about with troll-my-dames; I knew him once a servant of the Prince. I cannot tell, good sir, for which of his virtues it was, but
85   he was certainly whipt out of the court.

Clown

His vices, you would say; there's no virtue whipt out of the court. They cherish it to make it stay there; and yet it will no more but abide.

Autolycus

Vices, I would say, sir. I know this man well; he hath
90   been since an ape-bearer; then a process-server, a bailiff; then he compass'd a motion of the Prodigal Son, and married a tinker's wife within a mile where my land and living lies; and, having flown over many knavish professións, he settled only in rogue. Some call
95   him Autolycus.

Clown

Out upon him! prig, for my life, prig! He haunts wakes, fairs, and bear-baitings.

Autolycus

Very true, sir; he, sir, he; that's the rogue that put me into this apparel.

Clown

100   Not a more cowardly rogue in all Bohemia; if you had but look'd big and spit at him, he'd have run.

Autolycus

I must confess to you, sir, I am no fighter; I am false of heart that way; and that he knew, I warrant him.

Clown

How do you now?

Autolycus

105   Sweet sir, much better than I was; I can stand and walk. I will even take my leave of you and pace softly towards my kinsman's.

Clown

Shall I bring thee on the way?

Autolycus

No, good-fac'd sir; no, sweet sir.

Clown

Then fare thee well. I must go buy spices for our sheep- 110
shearing.

Autolycus

Prosper you, sweet sir! *[Exit* CLOWN.*]* Your purse is not
hot enough to purchase your spice. I'll be with you at
your sheep-shearing too. If I make not this cheat bring
out another, and the shearers prove sheep, let me be 115
unroll'd, and my name put in the book of virtue! *[Sings.]*

> Jog on, jog on, the footpath way,
>   And merrily hent the stile-a;
> A merry heart goes all the day,
>   Your sad tires in a mile-a.   120

[Exit.]

Scene IV

Bohemia. The shepherd's cottage.

[Enter FLORIZEL and PERDITA.]

Florizel

These your unusual weeds to each part of you
Do give a life – no shepherdess, but Flora
Peering in April's front. This your sheep-shearing
Is as a meeting of the petty gods,
And you the Queen on't.

Perdita

5   Sir, my gracious lord,
To chide at your extremes it not becomes me –
O, pardon that I name them! Your high self,
The gracious mark o' th' land, you have obscur'd
With a swain's wearing; and me, poor lowly maid,
10 Most goddess-like prank'd up. But that our feasts
In every mess have folly, and the feeders
Digest it with a custom, I should blush
To see you so attir'd; swoon, I think,
To show myself a glass.

Florizel

                 I bless the time
15 When my good falcon made her flight across
Thy father's ground.

Perdita

                 Now Jove afford you cause!
To me the difference forges dread; your greatness
Hath not been us'd to fear. Even now I tremble
To think your father, by some accident,
20 Should pass this way, as you did. O, the Fates!
How would he look to see his work, so noble,
Vilely bound up? What would he say? Or how
Should I, in these my borrowed flaunts, behold
The sternness of his presence?

Florizel

                                    Apprehend

Nothing but jollity. The gods themselves,   25
Humbling their deities to love, have taken
The shapes of beasts upon them: Jupiter
Became a bull and bellow'd; the green Neptune
A ram and bleated; and the fire-rob'd god,
Golden Apollo, a poor humble swain,   30
As I seem now. Their transformations
Were never for a piece of beauty rarer,
Nor in a way so chaste, since my desires,
Run not before mine honour, nor my lusts
Burn hotter than my faith.

Perdita

                                    O, but, sir,   35

Your resolution cannot hold when 'tis
Oppos'd, as it must be, by th' pow'r of the King.
One of these two must be necessities,
Which then will speak, that you must change this
        purpose,
Or I my life.

Florizel

                    Thou dearest Perdita,   40

With these forc'd thoughts, I prithee, darken not
The mirth o' th' feast. Or I'll be thine, my fair,
Or not my father's; for I cannot be
Mine own, nor anything to any, if
I be not thine. To this I am most constant,   45
Though destiny say no. Be merry, gentle;
Strangle such thoughts as these with any thing
That you behold the while. Your guests are coming.
Lift up your countenance, as it were the day
Of celebration of that nuptial which   50
We two have sworn shall come.

Perdita

                                    O Lady Fortune,

Stand you auspicious!

Florizel

See, your guests approach.
Address yourself to entertain them sprightly,
And let's be red with mirth.

[*Enter* SHEPHERD, *with* POLIXENES *and* CAMILLO,
disguised; CLOWN, MOPSA, DORCAS, *with Others.*]

Shepherd

55   Fie, daughter! When my old wife liv'd, upon
This day she was both pantler, butler, cook;
Both dame and servant; welcom'd all; serv'd all;
Would sing her song and dance her turn; now here
At upper end o' th' table, now i' th' middle;
60   On his shoulder, and his; her face o' fire
With labour, and the thing she took to quench it
She would to each one sip. You are retired,
As if you were a feasted one, and not
The hostess of the meeting. Pray you bid
65   These unknown friends to's welcome, for it is
A way to make us better friends, more known.
Come, quench your blushes, and present yourself
That which you are, Mistress o' th' Feast. Come on,
And bid us welcome to your sheep-shearing,
As your good flock shall prosper.

Perdita

70   [*To* POLIXENES]   Sir, welcome.
It is my father's will I should take on me
The hostess-ship o' th' day. [*To* CAMILLO] You're
    welcome, sir.
Give me those flow'rs there, Dorcas. Reverend sirs,
For you there's rosemary and rue; these keep
75   Seeming and savour all the winter long.
Grace and remembrance be to you both!
And welcome to our shearing.

Polixenes

Shepherdess –
A fair one are you – well you fit our ages

With flow'rs of winter.

Perdita

Sir, the year growing ancient,
Not yet on summer's death nor on the birth   80
Of trembling winter, the fairest flow'rs o' th' season
Are our carnations and streak'd gillyvors,
Which some call nature's bastards. Of that kind
Our rustic garden's barren; and I care not
To get slips of them.

Polixenes

Wherefore, gentle maiden,   85
Do you neglect them?

Perdita

For I have heard it said
There is an art which in their piedness shares
With great creating nature.

Polixenes

Say there be;
Yet nature is made better by no mean
But nature makes that mean; so over that art,   90
Which you say adds to nature, is an art
That nature makes. You see, sweet maid, we marry
A gentler scion to the wildest stock,
And make conceive a bark of baser kind
By bud of nobler race. This is an art   95
Which does mend nature – change it rather; but
The art itself is nature.

Perdita

So it is.

Polixenes

Then make your garden rich in gillyvors,
And do not call them bastards.

Perdita

I'll not put
The dibble in earth to set one slip of them;   100
No more than were I painted I would wish
This youth should say 'twere well, and only therefore

        Desire to breed by me. Here's flow'rs for you:
        Hot lavender, mints, savory, marjoram;
105   The marigold, that goes to bed wi' th' sun,
        And with him rises weeping; these are flow'rs
        Of middle summer, and I think they are given
        To men of middle age. Y'are very welcome.

Camillo

        I should leave grazing, were I of your flock,
        And only live by gazing.

Perdita

110   Out, alas!
        You'd be so lean that blasts of January
        Would blow you through and through. Now, my
           fair'st friend,
        I would I had some flow'rs o' th' spring that might
        Become your time of day – and yours, and yours,
115   That wear upon your virgin branches yet
        Your maidenheads growing. O Proserpina,
        For the flowers now that, frighted, thou let'st fall
        From Dis's waggon! – daffodils,
        That come before the swallow dares, and take
120   The winds of March with beauty; violets, dim
        But sweeter than the lids of Juno's eyes
        Or Cytherea's breath; pale primroses,
        That die unmarried ere they can behold
        Bright Phoebus in his strength – a malady
125   Most incident to maids; bold oxlips, and
        The crown-imperial; lilies of all kinds,
        The flow'r-de-luce being one. O, these I lack
        To make you garlands of, and my sweet friend
        To strew him o'er and o'er!

Florizel

                  What, like a corse?

Perdita

130   No; like a bank for love to lie and play on;
        Not like a corse; or if – not to be buried,
        But quick, and in mine arms. Come, take your flow'rs.

Methinks I play as I have seen them do
In Whitsun pastorals. Sure, this robe of mine
Does change my disposition.

Florizel

What you do   135
Still betters what is done. When you speak, sweet,
I'd have you do it ever. When you sing,
I'd have you buy and sell so; so give alms;
Pray so; and, for the ord'ring your affairs,
To sing them too. When you do dance, I wish you   140
A wave o' th' sea, that you might ever do
Nothing but that; move still, still so,
And own no other function. Each your doing,
So singular in each particular,
Crowns what you are doing in the present deeds,   145
That all your acts are queens.

Perdita

O Doricles,
Your praises are too large. But that your youth,
And the true blood which peeps fairly through't,
Do plainly give you out an unstain'd shepherd,
With wisdom I might fear, my Doricles,   150
You woo'd me the false way.

Florizel

I think you have
As little skill to fear as I have purpose
To put you to't. But, come; our dance, I pray.
Your hand, my Perdita; so turtles pair
That never mean to part.

Perdita

I'll swear for 'em.   155

Polixenes

This is the prettiest low-born lass that ever
Ran on the green-sward; nothing she does or seems
But smacks of something greater than herself,
Too noble for this place.

Camillo

He tells her something
160 That makes her blood look out. Good sooth, she is
The queen of curds and cream.

Clown

Come on, strike up.

Dorcas

Mopsa must be your mistress; marry, garlic,
To mend her kissing with!

Mopsa

Now, in good time!

Clown

Not a word, a word; we stand upon our manners.
165 Come, strike up.   [*Music.*]

[*Here a dance of Shepherds and Shepherdesses.*]

Polixenes

Pray, good shepherd, what fair swain is this
Which dances with your daughter?

Shepherd

They call him Doricles, and boasts himself
To have a worthy feeding; but I have it
170 Upon his own report, and I believe it:
He looks like sooth. He says he loves my daughter;
I think so too; for never gaz'd the moon
Upon the water as he'll stand and read,
As 'twere, my daughter's eyes; and, to be plain,
175 I think there is not half a kiss to choose
Who loves another best.

Polixenes

She dances featly.

Shepherd

So she does any thing; though I report it
That should be silent. If young Doricles
Do light upon her, she shall bring him that
180 Which he not dreams of.

[*Enter a Servant.*]

Servant

O master, if you did but hear the pedlar at the door,
you would never dance again after a tabor and pipe; no,
the bagpipe could not move you. He sings several tunes
faster than you'll tell money; he utters them as he had
eaten ballads, and all men's ears grew to his tunes.   185

Clown

He could never come better; he shall come in. I love a
ballad but even too well, if it be doleful matter merrily
set down, or a very pleasant thing indeed and sung
lamentally.

Servant

He hath songs for man or woman of all sizes; no 190
milliner can so fit his customers with gloves. He has
the prettiest love-songs for maids; so without bawdry,
which is strange; with such delicate burdens of dildos
and fadings, 'jump her and thump her'; and where
some stretch-mouth'd rascal would, as it were, mean 195
mischief, and break a foul gap into the matter, he
makes the maid to answer 'Whoop, do me no harm,
good man' – puts him off, slights him, with 'Whoop,
do me no harm, good man'.

Polixenes

This is a brave fellow.   200

Clown

Believe me, thou talkest of an admirable conceited
fellow. Has he any unbraided wares?

Servant

He hath ribbons of all the colours i' th' rainbow; points,
more than all the lawyers in Bohemia can learnedly
handle, though they come to him by th' gross; inkles, 205
caddisses, cambrics, lawns. Why he sings 'em over as
they were gods or goddesses; you would think a smock
were a she-angel, he so chants to the sleevehand and
the work about the square on't.

Clown

Prithee bring him in; and let him approach singing.   210

Perdita

Forewarn him that he use no scurrilous words in's tunes.   *[Exit Servant.]*

Clown

You have of these pedlars that have more in them than you'd think, sister.

Perdita

215   Ay, good brother, or go about to think.

[Enter AUTOLYCUS, *singing:]*

Lawn as white as driven snow;
Cypress black as e'er was crow;
Gloves as sweet as damask roses;
Masks for faces and for noses;
220   Bugle bracelet, necklace amber,
Perfume for a lady's chamber;
Golden quoifs and stomachers,
For my lads to give their dears;
Pins and poking-sticks of steel –
225   What maids lack from head to heel.
Come, buy of me, come; come buy, come buy;
Buy, lads, or else your lasses cry.
Come, buy.

Clown

If I were not in love with Mopsa, thou shouldst take no
230   money of me; but being enthrall'd as I am, it will also be the bondage of certain ribbons and gloves.

Mopsa

I was promis'd them against the feast; but they come not too late now.

Dorcas

He hath promis'd you more than that, or there be liars.

Mopsa

235   He hath paid you all he promis'd you. May be he has paid you more, which will shame you to give him again.

Clown

Is there no manners left among maids? Will they wear their plackets where they should bear their faces? Is there not milking-time, when you are going to bed, or 240 kiln-hole, to whistle off these secrets, but you must be tittle-tattling before all our our guests? 'Tis well they are whisp'ring. Clammer your tongues, and not a word more.

Mopsa

I have done. Come, you promis'd me a tawdry-lace, 245 and a pair of sweet gloves.

Clown

Have I not told thee how I was cozen'd by the way, and lost all my money?

Autolycus

And indeed, sir, there are cozeners abroad; therefore it behoves men to be wary. 250

Clown

Fear not thou, man; thou shalt lose nothing here.

Autolycus

I hope so, sir; for I have about me many parcels of charge.

Clown

What hast here? Ballads?

Mopsa

Pray now, buy some. I love a ballad in print a-life, for then we are sure they are true. 255

Autolycus

Here's one to a very doleful tune: how a usurer's wife was brought to bed of twenty money-bags at a burden, and how she long'd to eat adders' heads and toads carbonado'd.

Mopsa

Is it true, think you? 260

Autolycus

Very true, and but a month old.

Dorcas

Bless me from marrying a usurer!

Autolycus

    Here's the midwife's name to't, one Mistress Taleporter,
and five or six honest wives that were present. Why

265   should I carry lies abroad?

Mopsa

    Pray you now, buy it.

Clown

    Come on, lay it by; and let's first see moe ballads; we'll
buy the other things anon.

Autolycus

    Here's another ballad, of a fish that appeared upon

270   the coast on Wednesday the fourscore of April, forty
thousand fathom above water, and sung this ballad
against the hard hearts of maids. It was thought she
was a woman, and was turn'd into a cold fish for she
would not exchange flesh with one that lov'd her. The

275   ballad is very pitiful, and as true.

Dorcas

    Is it true too, think you?

Autolycus

    Five justices' hands at it; and witnesses more than my
pack will hold.

Clown

    Lay it by too. Another.

Autolycus

280   This is a merry ballad, but a very pretty one.

Mopsa

    Let's have some merry ones.

Autolycus

    Why, this is a passing merry one, and goes to the tune
of 'Two maids wooing a man.' There's scarce a maid
westward but she sings it; 'tis in request, I can tell

285   you.

Mopsa

    We can both sing it. If thou'lt bear a part, thou shalt
hear; 'tis in three parts.

Dorcas

    We had the tune on't a month ago.

Autolycus

    I can bear my part; you must know 'tis my occupation.
    Have at it with you.   290

[Song.]

Autolycus

      Get you hence, for I must go
      Where it fits not you to know.

Dorcas

      Whither?

Mopsa

          O, whither?

Dorcas

              Whither?

Mopsa

      It becomes thy oath full well
      Thou to me thy secrets tell.   295

Dorcas

      Me too! Let me go thither.

Mopsa

      Or thou goest to th' grange or mill.

Dorcas

      If to either, thou dost ill.

Autolycus

      Neither.

Dorcas

          What, neither?

Autolycus

              Neither.

Dorcas

      Thou hast sworn my love to be.   300

Mopsa

      Thou hast sworn it more to me.
      Then whither goest? Say, whither?

Clown

We'll have this song out anon by ourselves; my father
and the gentlemen are in sad talk, and we'll not trouble
305 them. Come, bring away thy pack after me. Wenches,
I'll buy for you both. Pedlar, let's have the first choice.
Follow me, girls.   *[Exit with* DORCAS *and* MOPSA.*]*

Autolycus

And you shall pay well for 'em.

[Exit AUTOLYCUS, *singing:]*

>   Will you buy any tape,
> 310   Or lace for your cape,
>   My dainty duck, my dear-a?
>   Any silk, any thread,
>   Any toys for your head,
>   Of the new'st and fin'st, fin'st wear-a?
> 315   Come to the pedlar;
>   Money's a meddler
>   That doth utter all men's ware-a.

[Re-enter Servant.]

Servant

Master, there is three carters, three shepherds, three
neat-herds, three swine-herds, that have made
320 themselves all men of hair; they call themselves
Saltiers, and they have a dance which the wenches say
is a gallimaufry of gambols, because they are not in't;
but they themselves are o' th' mind, if it be not too
rough for some that know little but bowling, it will
325 please plentifully.

Shepherd

Away! We'll none on't; here has been too much homely
foolery already. I know, sir, we weary you.

Polixenes

You weary those that refresh us. Pray, let's see these four
threes of herdsmen.

Servant

One three of them, by their own report, sir, hath 330
danc'd before the King; and not the worst of the three
but jumps twelve foot and a half by th' squier.

Shepherd

Leave your prating; since these good men are pleas'd,
let them come in; but quickly now.

Servant

Why, they stay at door, sir.   *[Exit.]* 335

[Here a Dance of twelve Satyrs.]

Polixenes

[To SHEPHERD*]* O, father, you'll know more of that
    hereafter.
[To CAMILLO*]* Is it not too far gone? 'Tis time to part
    them.
He's simple and tells much. *[To* FLORIZEL*]* How now,
    fair shepherd!
Your heart is full of something that does take
Your mind from feasting. Sooth, when I was young 340
And handed love as you do, I was wont
To load my she with knacks; I would have ransack'd
The pedlar's silken treasury and have pour'd it
To her acceptance: you have let him go
And nothing marted with him. If your lass 345
Interpretation should abuse and call this
Your lack of love or bounty, you were straited
For a reply, at least if you make a care
Of happy holding her.

Florizel

                    Old sir, I know
She prizes not such trifles as these are. 350
The gifts she looks from me are pack'd and lock'd
Up in my heart, which I have given already,
But not deliver'd. O, hear me breathe my life
Before this ancient sir, whom, it should seem,
Hath sometime lov'd. I take thy hand – this hand, 355

As soft as dove's down and as white as it,
Or Ethiopian's tooth, or the fann'd snow that's bolted
By th' northern blasts twice o'er.

Polixenes

What follows this?
How prettily the young swain seems to wash
360   The hand was fair before! I have put you out.
But to your protestation; let me hear
What you profess.

Florizel

Do, and be witness to't.

Polixenes
And this my neighbour too?

Florizel

And he, and more
Than he, and men – the earth, the heavens, and all:
365   That, were I crown'd the most imperial monarch,
Thereof most worthy, were I the fairest youth
That ever made eye swerve, had force and knowledge
More than was ever man's, I would not prize them
Without her love; for her employ them all;
370   Commend them and condemn them to her service
Or to their own perdition.

Polixenes

Fairly offer'd.

Camillo
This shows a sound affection.

Shepherd

But, my daughter,
Say you the like to him?

Perdita

I cannot speak
So well, nothing so well; no, nor mean better.
375   By th' pattern of mine own thoughts I cut out
The purity of his.

Shepherd

Take hands, a bargain!

And, friends unknown, you shall bear witness to't:
I give my daughter to him, and will make
Her portion equal his.

Florizel

           O, that must be
I' th' virtue of your daughter. One being dead,   380
I shall have more than you can dream of yet;
Enough then for your wonder. But come on,
Contract us fore these witnesses.

Shepherd

                Come, your hand;
And, daughter, yours.

Polixenes

              Soft, swain, awhile, beseech you;
Have you a father?

Florizel

            I have, but what of him?   385

Polixenes

Knows he of this?

Florizel

           He neither does nor shall.

Polixenes

Methinks a father
Is at the nuptial of his son a guest
That best becomes the table. Pray you, once more,
Is not your father grown incapable   390
Of reasonable affairs? Is he not stupid
With age and alt'ring rheums? Can he speak, hear,
Know man from man, dispute his own estate?
Lies he not bed-rid, and again does nothing
But what he did being childish?

Florizel

               No, good sir;   395
He has his health, and ampler strength indeed
Than most have of his age.

Polixenes

           By my white beard,

You offer him, if this be so, a wrong
Something unfilial. Reason my son
400 Should choose himself a wife; but as good reason
The father – all whose joy is nothing else
But fair posterity – should hold some counsel
In such a business.

Florizel

I yield all this;
But, for some other reasons, my grave sir,
405 Which 'tis not fit you know, I not acquaint
My father of this business.

Polixenes

Let him know't.

Florizel

He shall not.

Polixenes

Prithee let him.

Florizel

No, he must not.

Shepherd

Let him, my son; he shall not need to grieve
At knowing of thy choice.

Florizel

Come, come, he must not.
Mark our contract.

Polixenes

410 *[Discovering himself]* Mark your divorce, young sir,
Whom son I dare not call; thou art too base
To be acknowledg'd – thou a sceptre's heir,
That thus affects a sheep-hook! Thou, old traitor,
I am sorry that by hanging thee I can but
415 Shorten thy life one week. And thou, fresh piece
Of excellent witchcraft, who of force must know
The royal fool thou cop'st with –

Shepherd

O, my heart!

Polixenes

    I'll have thy beauty scratch'd with briers and made
    More homely than thy state. For thee, fond boy,
    If I may ever know thou dost but sigh   420
    That thou no more shalt see this knack – as never
    I mean thou shalt – we'll bar thee from succession;
    Not hold thee of our blood, no, not our kin,
    Farre than Deucalion off. Mark thou my words.
    Follow us to the court. Thou churl, for this time,   425
    Though full of our displeasure, yet we free thee
    From the dead blow of it. And you, enchantment,
    Worthy enough a herdsman – yea, him too
    That makes himself, but for our honour therein,
    Unworthy thee – if ever henceforth thou   430
    These rural latches to his entrance open,
    Or hoop his body more with thy embraces,
    I will devise a death as cruel for thee
    As thou art tender to't.   *[Exit.]*

Perdita

                Even here undone!
    I was not much afeard; for once or twice   435
    I was about to speak and tell him plainly
    The self-same sun that shines upon his court
    Hides not his visage from our cottage, but
    Looks on alike. *[To* FLORIZEL*]* Will't please you, sir, be
        gone?
    I told you what would come of this. Beseech you,   440
    Of your own state take care. This dream of mine –
    Being now awake, I'll queen it no inch farther,
    But milk my ewes and weep.

Camillo

                Why, how now, father!
    Speak ere thou diest.

Shepherd

            I cannot speak nor think,
    Nor dare to know that which I know. *[To* FLORIZEL*]*
        O sir,   445

You have undone a man of fourscore-three
That thought to fill his grave in quiet, yea,
To die upon the bed my father died,
To lie close by his honest bones; but now
450   Some hangman must put on my shroud and lay me
Where no priest shovels in dust. *[To* PERDITA*]* O cursed
    wretch,
That knew'st this was the Prince, and wouldst
    adventure
To mingle faith with him! – Undone, undone!
If I might die within this hour, I have liv'd
To die when I desire.   *[Exit.]*

Florizel
455   Why look you so upon me?
I am but sorry, not afeard; delay'd,
But nothing alt'red. What I was, I am:
More straining on for plucking back; not following
My leash unwillingly.

Camillo
                  Gracious, my lord,
460   You know your father's temper. At this time
He will allow no speech – which I do guess
You do not purpose to him – and as hardly
Will he endure your sight as yet, I fear;
Then, till the fury of his Highness settle,
Come not before him.

Florizel
465   I not purpose it.
I think Camillo?

Camillo
                Even he, my lord.

Perdita
How often have I told you 'twould be thus!
How often said my dignity would last
But till 'twere known!

Florizel
                It cannot fail but by

The violation of my faith; and then   470
Let nature crush the sides o' th' earth together
And mar the seeds within! Lift up thy looks.
From my succession wipe me, father; I
Am heir to my affection.

Camillo

                Be advis'd.

Florizel

I am – and by my fancy; if my reason   475
Will thereto be obedient, I have reason;
If not, my senses, better pleas'd with madness,
Do bid it welcome.

Camillo

              This is desperate, sir.

Florizel

So call it; but it does fulfil my vow:
I needs must think it honesty. Camillo,   480
Not for Bohemia, nor the pomp that may
Be thereat glean'd, for all the sun sees or
The close earth wombs, or the profound seas hides
In unknown fathoms, will I break my oath
To this my fair belov'd. Therefore, I pray you,   485
As you have ever been my father's honour'd friend,
When he shall miss me – as, in faith, I mean not
To see him any more – cast your good counsels
Upon his passion. Let myself and Fortune
Tug for the time to come. This you may know,   490
And so deliver: I am put to sea
With her who here I cannot hold on shore.
And most opportune to her need I have
A vessel rides fast by, but not prepar'd
For this design. What course I mean to hold   495
Shall nothing benefit your knowledge, nor
Concern me the reporting.

Camillo

              O my lord,
I would your spirit were easier for advice,

Or stronger for your need.
Florizel

Hark, Perdita.

[Takes her aside.]

[To CAMILLO*]* I'll hear you by and by.
Camillo

He's irremovable,

500 Resolv'd for flight. Now were I happy if
His going I could frame to serve my turn,
Save him from danger, do him love and honour,
Purchase the sight again of dear Sicilia
505 And that unhappy king, my master, whom
I so much thirst to see.
Florizel

Now, good Camillo,

I am so fraught with curious business that
I leave out ceremony.
Camillo

Sir, I think

You have heard of my poor services i' th' love
That I have borne your father?
Florizel

510 Very nobly

Have you deserv'd. It is my father's music
To speak your deeds; not little of his care
To have them recompens'd as thought on.
Camillo

Well, my lord,

If you may please to think I love the King,
515 And through him what's nearest to him, which is
Your gracious self, embrace but my direction.
If your more ponderous and settled project
May suffer alteration, on mine honour,
I'll point you where you shall have such receiving
520 As shall become your Highness; where you may
Enjoy your mistress, from the whom, I see,
There's no disjunction to be made but by,

As heavens forfend! your ruin – marry her;
And with my best endeavours in your absence
Your discontenting father strive to qualify,   525
And bring him up to liking.

Florizel
                              How, Camillo,
May this, almost a miracle, be done?
That I may call thee something more than man,
And after that trust to thee.

Camillo
                              Have you thought on
A place whereto you'll go?

Florizel
                              Not any yet;   530
But as th' unthought-on accident is guilty
To what we wildly do, so we profess
Ourselves to be the slaves of chance and flies
Of every wind that blows.

Camillo
                              Then list to me.
This follows, if you will not change your purpose   535
But undergo this flight: make for Sicilia,
And there present yourself and your fair princess –
For so, I see, she must be – fore Leontes.
She shall be habited as it becomes
The partner of your bed. Methinks I see   540
Leontes opening his free arms and weeping
His welcomes forth; asks thee there 'Son, forgiveness!'
As 'twere i' th' father's person; kisses the hands
Of your fresh princess; o'er and o'er divides him
'Twixt his unkindness and his kindness – th'one   545
He chides to hell, and bids the other grow
Faster than thought or time.

Florizel
                              Worthy Camillo,
What colour for my visitation shall I
Hold up before him?

Camillo

                         Sent by the King your father
550   To greet him and to give him comforts. Sir,
      The manner of your bearing towards him, with
      What you as from your father shall deliver,
      Things known betwixt us three, I'll write you down;
      The which shall point you forth at every sitting
555   What you must say, that he shall not perceive
      But that you have your father's bosom there
      And speak his very heart.

Florizel

                        I am bound to you.
      There is some sap in this.

Camillo

                       A course more promising
      Than a wild dedication of yourselves
560   To unpath'd waters, undream'd shores, most certain
      To miseries enough; no hope to help you,
      But as you shake off one to take another;
      Nothing so certain as your anchors, who
      Do their best office if they can but stay you
565   Where you'll be loath to be. Besides, you know
      Prosperity's the very bond of love,
      Whose fresh complexion and whose heart together
      Affliction alters.

Perdita

                    One of these is true:
      I think affliction may subdue the cheek,
      But not take in the mind.

Camillo

570   Yea, say you so?
      There shall not at your father's house these seven
          years
      Be born another such.

Florizel

                   My good Camillo,
      She is as forward of her breeding as

She is i' th' rear o' our birth.

Camillo

      I cannot say 'tis pity
She lacks instructions, for she seems a mistress   575
To most that teach.

Perdita

     Your pardon, sir; for this
I'll blush you thanks.

Florizel

      My prettiest Perdita!
But, O, the thorns we stand upon! Camillo –
Preserver of my father, now of me;
The medicine of our house – how shall we do?   580
We are not furnish'd like Bohemia's son;
Nor shall appear in Sicilia.

Camillo

      My lord,
Fear none of this. I think you know my fortunes
Do all lie there. It shall be so my care
To have you royally appointed as if   585
The scene you play were mine. For instance, sir,
That you may know you shall not want – one word.

          [They talk aside.]

[Re-enter AUTOLYCUS.*]*

Autolycus

Ha, ha! what a fool Honesty is! and Trust, his sworn
brother, a very simple gentleman! I have sold all my
trumpery; not a counterfeit stone, not a ribbon, glass, 590
pomander, brooch, table-book, ballad, knife, tape,
glove, shoe-tie, bracelet, horn-ring, to keep my pack
from fasting. They throng who should buy first, as if my
trinkets had been hallowed and brought a benediction
to the buyer; by which means I saw whose purse was 595
best in picture; and what I saw, to my good use I
remem'bred. My clown, who wants but something to
be a reasonable man, grew so in love with the wenches'

song that he would not stir his pettitoes till he had
600 both tune and words, which so drew the rest of the
herd to me that all their other senses stuck in ears. You
might have pinch'd a placket, it was senseless; 'twas
nothing to geld a codpiece of a purse; I would have fil'd
keys off that hung in chains. No hearing, no feeling,
605 but my sir's song, and admiring the nothing of it. So
that in this time of lethargy I pick'd and cut most of
their festival purses; and had not the old man come in
with a whoobub against his daughter and the King's
son and scar'd my choughs from the chaff, I had not
610 left a purse alive in the whole army.

[CAMILLO, FLORIZEL, *and* PERDITA, *come forward.*]

Camillo
Nay, but my letters, by this means being there
So soon as you arrive, shall clear that doubt.
Florizel
And those that you'll procure from King Leontes?
Camillo
Shall satisfy your father.
Perdita
               Happy be you!
All that you speak shows fair.
Camillo
615 *[Seeing* AUTOLYCUS*]*   Who have we here?
We'll make an instrument of this; omit
Nothing may give us aid.
Autolycus
[Aside] If they have overheard me now – why, hanging.
Camillo
How now, good fellow! Why shak'st thou so? Fear not,
620 man; here's no harm intended to thee.
Autolycus
I am a poor fellow, sir.
Camillo
Why, be so still; here's nobody will steal that from thee.

Yet for the outside of thy poverty we must make an
exchange; therefore disease thee instantly – thou must
think there's a necessity in't – and change garments 625
with this gentleman. Though the pennyworth on his
side be the worst, yet hold thee, there's some boot.

[Giving money.]

Autolycus
I am a poor fellow, sir. *[Aside]* I know ye well enough.
Camillo
Nay, prithee dispatch. The gentleman is half flay'd
already. 630
Autolycus
Are you in earnest, sir? *[Aside]* I smell the trick on't.
Florizel
Dispatch, I prithee.
Autolycus
Indeed, I have had earnest; but I cannot with conscience
take it.
Camillo
Unbuckle, unbuckle. 635

[FLORIZEL and AUTOLYCUS exchange garments.]

Fortunate mistress – let my prophecy
Come home to ye! – you must retire yourself
Into some covert; take your sweetheart's hat
And pluck it o'er your brows, muffle your face,
Dismantle you, and, as you can, disliken 640
The truth of your own seeming, that you may –
For I do fear eyes over – to shipboard
Get undescried.
Perdita
     I see the play so lies
That I must bear a part.
Camillo
      No remedy.
Have you done there?

Florizel

645   Should I now meet my father,
    He would not call me son.

Camillo

                                Nay, you shall have no hat.

[Giving it to PERDITA.*]*

    Come, lady, come. Farewell, my friend.

Autolycus

                                Adieu, sir.

Florizel

    O Perdita, what have we twain forgot!
    Pray you a word.   *[They converse apart.]*

Camillo

650   *[Aside]* What I do next shall be to tell the King
    Of this escape, and whither they are bound;
    Wherein my hope is I shall so prevail
    To force him after; in whose company
    I shall re-view Sicilia, for whose sight
    I have a woman's longing.

Florizel

655   Fortune speed us!
    Thus we set on, Camillo, to th' sea-side.

Camillo

    The swifter speed the better.

[Exeunt FLORIZEL, PERDITA, *and* CAMILLO.*]*

Autolycus

    I understand the business, I hear it. To have an open
    ear, a quick eye, and a nimble hand, is necessary for
660   a cut-purse; a good nose is requisite also, to smell out
    work for th' other senses. I see this is the time that
    the unjust man doth thrive. What an exchange had
    this been without boot! What a boot is here with this
    exchange! Sure, the gods do this year connive at us, and
665   we may do anything extempore. The Prince himself is
    about a piece of iniquity – stealing away from his father

with his clog at his heels. If I thought it were a piece of
honesty to acquaint the King withal, I would not do't. I
hold it the more knavery to conceal it; and therein am
I constant to my profession.   670

[Re-enter CLOWN *and* SHEPHERD.*]*

Aside, aside – here is more matter for a hot brain. Every
lane's end, every shop, church, session, hanging, yields
a careful man work.

Clown

See, see; what a man you are now! There is no other
way but to tell the King she's a changeling and none of 675
your flesh and blood.

Shepherd

Nay, but hear me.

Clown

Nay – but hear me.

Shepherd

Go to, then.

Clown

She being none of your flesh and blood, your flesh and 680
blood has not offended the King; and so your flesh
and blood is not to be punish'd by him. Show those
things you found about her, those secret things – all
but what she has with her. This being done, let the law
go whistle; I warrant you.   685

Shepherd

I will tell the King all, every word – yea, and his son's
pranks too; who, I may say, is no honest man, neither
to his father nor to me, to go about to make me the
King's brother-in-law.

Clown

Indeed, brother-in-law was the farthest off you could 690
have been to him; and then your blood had been the
dearer by I know how much an ounce.

Autolycus

[Aside] Very wisely, puppies!

Shepherd

Well, let us to the King. There is that in this fardel will
695   make him scratch his beard.

Autolycus

[Aside] I know not what impediment this complaint
may be to the flight of my master.

Clown

Pray heartily he be at palace.

Autolycus

[Aside] Though I am not naturally honest, I am so
700   sometimes by chance. Let me pocket up my pedlar's
excrement. *[Takes off his false beard]* How now, rustics!
Whither are you bound?

Shepherd

To th' palace, an it like your worship.

Autolycus

Your affairs there, what, with whom, the condition of
705   that fardel, the place of your dwelling, your names,
your ages, of what having, breeding, and anything that
is fitting to be known – discover.

Clown

We are but plain fellows, sir.

Autolycus

A lie: you are rough and hairy. Let me have no lying;
710   it becomes none but tradesmen, and they often give us
soldiers the lie; but we pay them for it with stamped
coin, not stabbing steel; therefore they do not give us
the lie.

Clown

Your worship had like to have given us one, if you had
715   not taken yourself with the manner.

Shepherd

Are you a courtier, an't like you, sir?

Autolycus

Whether it like me or no, I am a courtier. Seest thou
not the air of the court in these enfoldings? Hath
not my gait in it the measure of the court? Receives

not thy nose court-odour from me? Reflect I not on 720
thy baseness court-contempt? Think'st thou, for that
I insinuate, that toaze from thee thy business, I am
therefore no courtier? I am courtier cap-a-pe, and one
that will either push on or pluck back thy business
there; whereupon I command thee to open thy affair. 725

Shepherd

My business, sir, is to the King.

Autolycus

What advocate hast thou to him?

Shepherd

I know not, an't like you.

Clown

Advocate's the court-word for a pheasant; say you have
none.

Shepherd

None, sir; I have no pheasant, cock nor hen. 730

Autolycus

How blessed are we that are not simple men!
Yet nature might have made me as these are,
Therefore I will not disdain.

Clown

This cannot be but a great courtier.

Shepherd

His garments are rich, but he wears them not 735
handsomely.

Clown

He seems to be the more noble in being fantastical.
A great man, I'll warrant; I know by the picking on's
teeth.

Autolycus

The fardel there? What's i' th' fardel? Wherefore that 740
box?

Shepherd

Sir, there lies such secrets in this fardel and box which
none must know but the King; and which he shall know
within this hour, if I may come to th' speech of him.

Autolycus

745   Age, thou hast lost thy labour.

Shepherd

    Why, sir?

Autolycus

    The King is not at the palace; he is gone aboard a new ship to purge melancholy and air himself; for, if thou be'st capable of things serious, thou must know the

750   King is full of grief.

Shepherd

    So 'tis said, sir – about his son, that should have married a shepherd's daughter.

Autolycus

    If that shepherd be not in handfast, let him fly; the curses he shall have, the tortures he shall feel, will

755   break the back of man, the heart of monster.

Clown

    Think you so, sir?

Autolycus

    Not he alone shall suffer what wit can make heavy and vengeance bitter; but those that are germane to him, though remov'd fifty times, shall all come under the

760   hangman – which, though it be great pity, yet it is necessary. An old sheep-whistling rogue, a ram-tender, to offer to have his daughter come into grace! Some say he shall be ston'd; but that death is too soft for him, say I. Draw our throne into a sheep-cote ! – all deaths are

765   too few, the sharpest too easy.

Clown

    Has the old man e'er a son, sir, do you hear, an't like you, sir?

Autolycus

    He has a son – who shall be flay'd alive; then 'nointed over with honey, set on the head of a wasp's nest;

770   then stand till he be three quarters and a dram dead; then recover'd again with aqua-vitae or some other hot infusion; then, raw as he is, and in the hottest

day prognostication proclaims, shall he be set against
a brick wall, the sun looking with a southward eye
upon him, where he is to behold him with flies blown 775
to death. But what talk we of these traitorly rascals,
whose miseries are to be smil'd at, their offences being
so capital? Tell me, for you seem to be honest plain
men, what you have to the King. Being something
gently consider'd, I'll bring you where he is aboard, 780
tender your persons to his presence, whisper him in
your behalfs; and if it be in man besides the King to
effect your suits, here is man shall do it.

Clown

He seems to be of great authority. Close with him, give
him gold; and though authority be a stubborn bear, yet 785
he is oft led by the nose with gold. Show the inside of
your purse to the outside of his hand, and no more ado.
Remember – ston'd and flay'd alive.

Shepherd

An't please you, sir, to undertake the business for us,
here is that gold I have. I'll make it as much more, and 790
leave this young man in pawn till I bring it you.

Autolycus

After I have done what I promised?

Shepherd

Ay, sir.

Autolycus

Well, give me the moiety. Are you a party in this
business?   795

Clown

In some sort, sir; but though my case be a pitiful one, I
hope I shall not be flay'd out of it.

Autolycus

O, that's the case of the shepherd's son! Hang him, he'll
be made an example.

Clown

Comfort, good comfort! We must to the King and show 800
our strange sights. He must know 'tis none of your

daughter nor my sister; we are gone else. Sir, I will give you as much as this old man does, when the business is performed; and remain, as he says, your pawn till it
805 be brought you.

Autolycus

I will trust you. Walk before toward the sea-side; go on the right-hand; I will but look upon the hedge, and follow you.

Clown

We are blest in this man, as I may say, even blest.

Shepherd

810 Let's before, as he bids us. He was provided to do us good.

[Exeunt SHEPHERD and CLOWN.]

Autolycus

If I had a mind to be honest, I see Fortune would not suffer me: she drops booties in my mouth. I am courted now with a double occasion – gold, and a means to
815 do the Prince my master good; which who knows how that may turn back to my advancement? I will bring these two moles, these blind ones, aboard him. If he think it fit to shore them again, and that the complaint they have to the King concerns him nothing, let him
820 call me rogue for being so far officious; for I am proof against that title, and what shame else belongs to't. To him will I present them. There may be matter in it.

[Exit.]

ACT FIVE

Scene I

Sicilia. The palace of Leontes.

[Enter LEONTES, CLEOMENES, DION, PAULINA, and Others.]

Cleomenes

    Sir, you have done enough, and have perform'd
    A saint-like sorrow. No fault could you make
    Which you have not redeem'd; indeed, paid down,
    More penitence than done trespass. At the last,
    Do as the heavens have done: forget your evil;   5
    With them forgive yourself.

Leontes

                    Whilst I remember
    Her and her virtues, I cannot forget
    My blemishes in them, and so still think of
    The wrong I did myself; which was so much
    That heirless it hath made my kingdom, and   10
    Destroy'd the sweet'st companion that e'er man
    Bred his hopes out of.

Paulina

                True, too true, my lord.
    If, one by one, you wedded all the world,
    Or from the all that are took something good
    To make a perfect woman, she you kill'd   15
    Would be unparallel'd.

Leontes

             I think so. Kill'd!
    She I kill'd! I did so; but thou strik'st me
    Sorely, to say I did. It is as bitter
    Upon thy tongue as in my thought. Now, good now,
    Say so but seldom.

Cleomenes

20   Not at all, good lady.
    You might have spoken a thousand things that
        would
    Have done the time more benefit, and grac'd
    Your kindness better.

Paulina

                              You are one of those
    Would have him wed again.

Dion

                                  If you would not so,
25 You pity not the state, nor the remembrance
    Of his most sovereign name; consider little
    What dangers, by his Highness' fail of issue,
    May drop upon his kingdom and devour
    Incertain lookers-on. What were more holy
30 Than to rejoice the former queen is well?
    What holier than, for royalty's repair,
    For present comfort, and for future good,
    To bless the bed of majesty again
    With a sweet fellow to't?

Paulina

                          There is none worthy,
35 Respecting her that's gone. Besides, the gods
    Will have fulfill'd their secret purposes;
    For has not the divine Apollo said,
    Is't not the tenour of his oracle,
    That King Leontes shall not have an heir
40 'Till his lost child be found? Which that it shall,
    Is all as monstrous to our human reason
    As my Antigonus to break his grave
    And come again to me; who, on my life,
    Did perish with the infant. 'Tis your counsel
45 My lord should to the heavens be contrary,
    Oppose against their wills. *[To* LEONTES*]* Care not for
        issue;
    The crown will find an heir. Great Alexander

Left his to th' worthiest; so his successor
Was like to be the best.

Leontes
                 Good Paulina,
Who hast the memory of Hermione,   50
I know, in honour, O that ever I
Had squar'd me to thy counsel! Then, even now,
I might have look'd upon my queen's full eyes,
Have taken treasure from her lips –

Paulina
                   And left them
More rich for what they yielded.

Leontes
                 Thou speak'st truth.   55
No more such wives; therefore, no wife. One worse,
And better us'd, would make her sainted spirit
Again possess her corpse, and on this stage,
Where we offend her now, appear soul-vex'd,
And begin 'Why to me' –

Paulina
                 Had she such power,   60
She had just cause.

Leontes
             She had; and would incense me
To murder her I married.

Paulina
               I should so.
Were I the ghost that walk'd, I'd bid you mark
Her eye, and tell me for what dull part in't
You chose her; then I'd shriek, that even your ears   65
Should rift to hear me; and the words that follow'd
Should be 'Remember mine'.

Leontes
                 Stars, stars,
And all eyes else dead coals! Fear thou no wife;
I'll have no wife, Paulina.

Paulina

                              Will you swear

70   Never to marry but by my free leave?

Leontes

    Never, Paulina; so be blest my spirit!

Paulina

    Then, good my lords, bear witness to his oath.

Cleomenes

    You tempt him over-much.

Paulina

                          Unless another,

    As like Hermione as is her picture,

    Affront his eye.

Cleomenes

             Good madam –

Paulina

75   I have done.

    Yet, if my lord will marry – if you will, sir,

    No remedy but you will – give me the office

    To choose you a queen. She shall not be so young

    As was your former; but she shall be such

80   As, walk'd your first queen's ghost, it should take joy

    To see her in your arms.

Leontes

                   My true Paulina,

    We shall not marry till thou bid'st us.

Paulina

                          That

    Shall be when your first queen's again in breath;

    Never till then.

[Enter a Gentleman.]

Gentleman

85   One that gives out himself Prince Florizel,

    Son of Polixenes, with his princess – she

    The fairest I have yet beheld – desires access

    To your high presence.

Leontes
                              What with him? He comes not
Like to his father's greatness. His approach,
So out of circumstance and sudden, tells us   90
'Tis not a visitation fram'd, but forc'd
By need and accident. What train?
Gentleman
                              But few,
And those but mean.
Leontes
                              His princess, say you, with him?
Gentleman
Ay; the most peerless piece of earth,
I think,
That e'er the sun shone bright on.
Paulina
                              O Hermione,   95
As every present time doth boast itself
Above a better gone, so must thy grave
Give way to what's seen now! Sir, you yourself
Have said and writ so, but your writing now
Is colder than that theme: 'She had not been,   100
Nor was not to be equall'd'. Thus your verse
Flow'd with her beauty once; 'tis shrewdly ebb'd,
To say you have seen a better.
Gentleman
                              Pardon, madam.
The one I have almost forgot – your pardon;
The other, when she has obtain'd your eye,   105
Will have your tongue too. This is a creature,
Would she begin a sect, might quench the zeal
Of all professors else, make proselytes
Of who she but bid follow.
Paulina
                              How! not women?
Gentleman
Women will love her that she is a woman   110

More worth than any man; men, that she is
The rarest of all women.

Leontes

       Go, Cleomenes;
Yourself, assisted with your honour'd friends,
Bring them to our embracement. *[Exeunt]* Still, 'tis
   strange
He thus should steal upon us.

Paulina

115   Had our prince,
Jewel of children, seen this hour, he had pair'd
Well with this lord; there was not full a month
Between their births.

Leontes

Prithee no more; cease. Thou know'st
120 He dies to me again when talk'd of. Sure,
When I shall see this gentleman, thy speeches
Will bring me to consider that which may
Unfurnish me of reason.

   [Re-enter CLEOMENES, *with* FLORIZEL, PERDITA, *and*
        Attendants.]

        They are come.
Your mother was most true to wedlock, Prince;
125 For she did print your royal father off,
Conceiving you. Were I but twenty-one,
Your father's image is so hit in you,
His very air, that I should call you brother,
As I did him, and speak of something wildly
130 By us perform'd before. Most dearly welcome!
And your fair princess – goddess! O, alas!
I lost a couple that 'twixt heaven and earth
Might thus have stood begetting wonder as
You, gracious couple, do. And then I lost –
135 All mine own folly – the society,
Amity too, of your brave father, whom,
Though bearing misery, I desire my life
Once more to look on him.

Florizel
                              By his command
Have I here touch'd Sicilia, and from him
Give you all greetings that a king, at friend,   140
Can send his brother; and, but infirmity,
Which waits upon worn times, hath something seiz'd
His wish'd ability, he had himself
The lands and waters 'twixt your throne and his
Measur'd, to look upon you; whom he loves,   145
He bade me say so, more than all the sceptres
And those that bear them living.

Leontes
                              O my brother –
Good gentleman! – the wrongs I have done thee stir
Afresh within me; and these thy offices,
So rarely kind, are as interpreters   150
Of my behind-hand slackness! Welcome hither,
As is the spring to th' earth. And hath he too
Expos'd this paragon to th' fearful usage,
At least ungentle, of the dreadful Neptune,
To greet a man not worth her pains, much less   155
Th' adventure of her person?

Florizel
                              Good, my lord,
She came from Libya.

Leontes
                              Where the warlike Smalus,
That noble honour'd lord, is fear'd and lov'd?

Florizel
Most royal sir, from thence; from him whose daughter
His tears proclaim'd his, parting with her; thence,   160
A prosperous south-wind friendly, we have cross'd,
To execute the charge my father gave me
For visiting your Highness. My best train
I have from your Sicilian shores dismiss'd;
Who for Bohemia bend, to signify   165
Not only my success in Libya, sir,

But my arrival and my wife's in safety
Here where we are.

Leontes

The blessed gods
Purge all infection from our air whilst you
170   Do climate here! You have a holy father,
A graceful gentleman, against whose person,
So sacred as it is, I have done sin,
For which the heavens, taking angry note,
Have left me issueless; and your father's blest,
175   As he from heaven merits it, with you,
Worthy his goodness. What might I have been,
Might I a son and daughter now have look'd on,
Such goodly things as you!

[Enter a Lord.]

Lord

Most noble sir,
That which I shall report will bear no credit,
180   Were not the proof so nigh. Please you, great sir,
Bohemia greets you from himself by me;
Desires you to attach his son, who has –
His dignity and duty both cast off –
Fled from his father, from his hopes, and with
A shepherd's daughter.

Leontes

185   Where's Bohemia? Speak.

Lord

Here in your city; I now came from him.
I speak amazedly; and it becomes
My marvel and my message. To your court
Whiles he was hast'ning – in the chase, it seems,
190   Of this fair couple – meets he on the way
The father of this seeming lady and
Her brother, having both their country quitted
With this young prince.

Florizel

                     Camillo has betray'd me;
Whose honour and whose honesty till now
Endur'd all weathers.

Lord

                   Lay't so to his charge;   195
He's with the King your father.

Leontes

                 Who? Camillo?

Lord

Camillo, sir; I spake with him; who now
Has these poor men in question. Never saw I
Wretches so quake. They kneel, they kiss the earth;
Forswear themselves as often as they speak.   200
Bohemia stops his ears, and threatens them
With divers deaths in death.

Perdita

               O my poor father!
The heaven sets spies upon us, will not have
Our contract celebrated.

Leontes

                You are married?

Florizel

We are not, sir, nor are we like to be;   205
The stars, I see, will kiss the valleys first.
The odds for high and low's alike.

Leontes

                    My lord,
Is this the daughter of a king?

Florizel

                 She is,
When once she is my wife.

Leontes

That 'once', I see by your good father's speed,   210
Will come on very slowly. I am sorry,
Most sorry, you have broken from his liking
Where you were tied in duty; and as sorry

Your choice is not so rich in worth as beauty,
That you might well enjoy her.

Florizel

215   Dear, look up.
Though Fortune, visible an enemy,
Should chase us with my father, pow'r no jot
Hath she to change our loves. Beseech you, sir,
Remember since you ow'd no more to time
220   Than I do now. With thought of such affections,
Step forth mine advocate; at your request
My father will grant precious things as trifles.

Leontes

Would he do so, I'd beg your precious mistress,
Which he counts but a trifle.

Paulina

                                 Sir, my liege,
225   Your eye hath too much youth in't. Not a month
Fore your queen died, she was more worth such gazes
Than what you look on now.

Leontes

                          I thought of her
Even in these looks I made. *[To* FLORIZEL*]* But your
   petition
Is yet unanswer'd. I will to your father.
230   Your honour not o'erthrown by your desires,
I am friend to them and you. Upon which errand
I now go toward him; therefore, follow me,
And mark what way I make. Come, good my lord.

[Exeunt.]

Scene II

Sicilia. Before the palace of Leontes.

[Enter AUTOLYCUS *and a Gentleman.]*

Autolycus
Beseech you, sir, were you present at this relation?
1 Gentleman
I was by the opening of the fardel, heard the old shepherd
deliver the manner how he found it; whereupon, after
a little amazedness, we were all commanded out of the
chamber; only this, methought I heard the shepherd   5
say he found the child.
Autolycus
I would most gladly know the issue of it.
1 Gentleman
I make a broken delivery of the business; but the changes
I perceived in the King and Camillo were very notes of
admiration. They seem'd almost, with staring on one   10
another, to tear the cases of their eyes; there was speech
in their dumbness, language in their very gesture; they
look'd as they had heard of a world ransom'd, or one
destroyed. A notable passion of wonder appeared in
them; but the wisest beholder that knew no more but   15
seeing could not say if th' importance were joy or sorrow
– but in the extremity of the one it must needs be.

[Enter another Gentleman.]

Here comes a gentleman that happily knows more. The
news, Rogero?
2 Gentleman
Nothing but bonfires. The oracle is fulfill'd: the King's   20
daughter is found. Such a deal of wonder is broken out
within this hour that ballad-makers cannot be able to
express it.

[Enter another Gentleman.]

Here comes the Lady Paulina's steward; he can deliver
25 you more. How goes it now, sir? This news, which is
call'd true, is so like an old tale that the verity of it is in
strong suspicion. Has the King found his heir?

3 *Gentleman*

Most true, if ever truth were pregnant by circumstance.
That which you hear you'll swear you see, there is such
30 unity in the proofs. The mantle of Queen Hermione's;
her jewel about the neck of it; the letters of Antigonus
found with it, which they know to be his character; the
majesty of the creature in resemblance of the mother;
the affection of nobleness which nature shows above
35 her breeding; and many other evidences – proclaim her
with all certainty to be the King's daughter. Did you see
the meeting of the two kings?

2 *Gentleman*

No.

3 *Gentleman*

Then have you lost a sight which was to be seen,
40 cannot be spoken of. There might you have beheld
one joy crown another, so and in such manner that it
seem'd sorrow wept to take leave of them; for their joy
waded in tears. There was casting up of eyes, holding
up of hands, with countenance of such distraction
45 that they were to be known by garment, not by favour.
Our king, being ready to leap out of himself for joy
of his found daughter, as if that joy were now become
a loss, cries 'O, thy mother, thy mother!' then asks
Bohemia forgiveness; then embraces his son-in-law;
50 then again worries he his daughter with clipping her.
Now he thanks the old shepherd, which stands by like
a weather-bitten conduit of many kings' reigns. I never
heard of such another encounter, which lames report
to follow it and undoes description to do it.

2 *Gentleman*

55 What, pray you, became of Antigonus, that carried
hence the child?

3 Gentleman

Like an old tale still, which will have matter to rehearse,
though credit be asleep and not an ear open: he was
torn to pieces with a bear. This avouches the shepherd's
son, who has not only his innocence, which seems   60
much, to justify him, but a handkerchief and rings of
his that Paulina knows.

1 Gentleman

What became of his bark and his followers?

3 Gentleman

Wreck'd the same instant of their master's death, and
in the view of the shepherd; so that all the instruments   65
which aided to expose the child were even then lost
when it was found. But, O, the noble combat that
'twixt joy and sorrow was fought in Paulina! She had
one eye declin'd for the loss of her husband, another
elevated that the oracle was fulfill'd. She lifted the   70
Princess from the earth, and so locks her in embracing
as if she would pin her to her heart, that she might no
more be in danger of losing.

1 Gentleman

The dignity of this act was worth the audience of kings
and princes; for by such was it acted.   75

3 Gentleman

One of the prettiest touches of all, and that which
angl'd for mine eyes – caught the water, though not
the fish – was, when at the relation of the Queen's
death, with the manner how she came to't bravely
confess'd and lamented by the King, how attentiveness   80
wounded his daughter; till from one sign of dolour to
another, she did with an 'Alas!' – I would fain say –
bleed tears; for I am sure my heart wept blood. Who
was most marble there changed colour; some swooned,
all sorrowed. If all the world could have seen't, the woe   85
had been universal.

1 Gentleman

Are they returned to the court?

3 *Gentleman*

No. The Princess hearing of her mother's statue, which is in the keeping of Paulina – a piece many years in
90 doing and now newly perform'd by that rare Italian master, Julio Romano, who, had he himself eternity and could put breath into his work, would beguile nature of her custom, so perfectly he is her ape. He so near to Hermione hath done Hermione that they say
95 one would speak to her and stand in hope of answer – thither with all greediness of affection are they gone, and there they intend to sup.

2 *Gentleman*

I thought she had some great matter there in hand; for she hath privately twice or thrice a day, ever since
100 the death of Hermione, visited that removed house. Shall we thither, and with our company piece the rejoicing?

1 *Gentleman*

Who would be thence that has the benefit of access? Every wink of an eye some new grace will be born. Our
105 absence makes us unthrifty to our knowledge. Let's along.

[Exeunt Gentlemen.]

Autolycus

Now, had I not the dash of my former life in me, would preferment drop on my head. I brought the old man and his son aboard the Prince; told him I heard them talk of a fardel and I know not what; but he at that
110 time over-fond of the shepherd's daughter – so he then took her to be – who began to be much sea-sick, and himself little better, extremity of weather continuing, this mystery remained undiscover'd. But 'tis all one to me; for had I been the finder-out of this secret, it would
115 not have relish'd among my other discredits.

[Enter SHEPHERD and CLOWN.]

Here come those I have done good to against my will, and already appearing in the blossoms of their fortune.

Shepherd

Come, boy; I am past moe children, but thy sons and daughters will be all gentlemen born.

Clown

You are well met, sir. You denied to fight with me this 120 other day, because I was no gentleman born. See you these clothes? Say you see them not and think me still no gentleman born. You were best say these robes are not gentlemen born. Give me the lie, do; and try whether I am not now a gentleman born. 125

Autolycus

I know you are now, sir, a gentleman born.

Clown

Ay, and have been so any time these four hours.

Shepherd

And so have I, boy.

Clown

So you have; but I was a gentleman born before my father; for the King's son took me by the hand and 130 call'd me brother; and then the two kings call'd my father brother; and then the Prince, my brother, and the Princess, my sister, call'd my father father. And so we wept; and there was the first gentleman-like tears that ever we shed. 135

Shepherd

We may live, son, to shed many more.

Clown

Ay; or else 'twere hard luck, being in so preposterous estate as we are.

Autolycus

I humbly beseech you, sir, to pardon me all the faults I have committed to your worship, and to give me your 140 good report to the Prince my master.

Shepherd

Prithee, son, do; for we must be gentle, now we are gentlemen.

Clown

Thou wilt amend thy life?

Autolycus

145   Ay, an it like your good worship.

Clown

Give me thy hand. I will swear to the Prince thou art as
honest a true fellow as any is in Bohemia.

Shepherd

You may say it, but not swear it.

Clown

Not swear it, now I am a gentleman? Let boors and
150   franklins say it: I'll swear it.

Shepherd

How if it be false, son?

Clown

If it be ne'er so false, a true gentleman may swear it
in the behalf of his friend. And I'll swear to the Prince
thou art a tall fellow of thy hands and that thou wilt
155   not be drunk; but I know thou art no tall fellow of thy
hands and that thou wilt be drunk. But I'll swear it;
and I would thou wouldst be a tall fellow of thy hands.

Autolycus

I will prove so, sir, to my power.

Clown

Ay, by any means, prove a tall fellow. If I do not wonder
160   how thou dar'st venture to be drunk not being a tall
fellow, trust me not. Hark! the kings and the princes,
our kindred, are going to see the Queen's picture.
Come, follow us; we'll be thy good masters.

[Exeunt.]

Scene III

Sicilia. A chapel in Paulina's house.

[Enter LEONTES, POLIXENES, FLORIZEL, PERDITA, CAMILLO, PAULINA, *Lords, and Attendants.]*

Leontes
    O grave and good Paulina, the great comfort
    That I have had of thee!

Paulina
                    What, sovereign sir,
    I did not well, I meant well. All my services
    You have paid home; but that you have vouchsaf'd
    With your crown'd brother and these your contracted   5
    Heirs of your kingdoms, my poor house to visit,
    It is a surplus of your grace, which never
    My life may last to answer.

Leontes
                 O Paulina,
    We honour you with trouble; but we came
    To see the statue of our queen. Your gallery   10
    Have we pass'd through, not without much content
    In many singularities; but we saw not
    That which my daughter came to look upon,
    The statue of her mother.

Paulina
               As she liv'd peerless,
    So her dead likeness, I do well believe,   15
    Excels whatever yet you look'd upon
    Or hand of man hath done; therefore I keep it
    Lonely, apart. But here it is. Prepare
    To see the life as lively mock'd as ever
    Still sleep mock'd death. Behold; and say 'tis well.   20

[PAULINE draws a curtain, and discovers HERMIONE standing like a statue.]

    I like your silence; it the more shows off

Your wonder; but yet speak. First, you, my liege.
Comes it not something near?

Leontes

                    Her natural posture!
Chide me, dear stone, that I may say indeed

25   Thou art Hermione; or rather, thou art she
In thy not chiding; for she was as tender
As infancy and grace. But yet, Paulina,
Hermione was not so much wrinkled, nothing
So aged as this seems.

Polixenes

               O, not by much!

Paulina

30   So much the more our carver's excellence,
Which lets go by some sixteen years and makes her
As she liv'd now.

Leontes

              As now she might have done,
So much to my good comfort as it is
Now piercing to my soul. O, thus she stood,

35   Even with such life of majesty – warm life,
As now it coldly stands – when first I woo'd her!
I am asham'd. Does not the stone rebuke me
For being more stone than it? O royal piece,
There's magic in thy majesty, which has

40   My evils conjur'd to remembrance, and
From thy admiring daughter took the spirits,
Standing like stone with thee!

Perdita

                    And give me leave,
And do not say 'tis superstition that
I kneel, and then implore her blessing. Lady,

45   Dear queen, that ended when I but began,
Give me that hand of yours to kiss.

Paulina

                   O, patience!
The statue is but newly fix'd, the colour's
Not dry.

Camillo
    My lord, your sorrow was too sore laid on,
    Which sixteen winters cannot blow away,   50
    So many summers dry. Scarce any joy
    Did ever so long live; no sorrow
    But kill'd itself much sooner.

Polixenes
                        Dear my brother,
    Let him that was the cause of this have pow'r
    To take off so much grief from you as he   55
    Will piece up in himself.

Paulina
                   Indeed, my lord,
    If I had thought the sight of my poor image
    Would thus have wrought you – for the stone is mine –
    I'd not have show'd it.

Leontes
                Do not draw the curtain.

Paulina
    No longer shall you gaze on't, lest your fancy   60
    May think anon it moves.

Leontes
                Let be, let be.
    Would I were dead, but that methinks already –
    What was he that did make it? See, my lord,
    Would you not deem it breath'd, and that those veins
    Did verily bear blood?

Polixenes
                Masterly done!   65
    The very life seems warm upon her lip.

Leontes
    The fixure of her eye has motion in't,
    As we are mock'd with art.

Paulina
               I'll draw the curtain.
    My lord's almost so far transported that
    He'll think anon it lives.

Leontes

70   O sweet Paulina,
Make me to think so twenty years together!
No settled senses of the world can match
The pleasure of that madness. Let't alone.

Paulina

I am sorry, sir, I have thus far stirr'd you; but
I could afflict you farther.

Leontes

75   Do, Paulina;
For this affliction has a taste as sweet
As any cordial comfort. Still, methinks,
There is an air comes from her. What fine chisel
Could ever yet cut breath? Let no man mock me,
For I will kiss her.

Paulina

80   Good my lord, forbear.
The ruddiness upon her lip is wet;
You'll mar it if you kiss it; stain your own
With oily painting. Shall I draw the curtain?

Leontes

No, not these twenty years.

Perdita

                        So long could I
Stand by, a looker-on.

Paulina

85   Either forbear,
Quit presently the chapel, or resolve you
For more amazement. If you can behold it,
I'll make the statue move indeed, descend,
And take you by the hand, but then you'll think –
90 Which I protest against – I am assisted
By wicked powers.

Leontes

               What you can make her do
I am content to look on; what to speak
I am content to hear; for 'tis as easy
To make her speak as move.

Paulina

It is requir'd
You do awake your faith. Then all stand still;   95
Or those that think it is unlawful business
I am about, let them depart.

Leontes

Proceed.
No foot shall stir.

Paulina

Music, awake her: strike.   *[Music.]*
'Tis time; descend; be stone no more; approach;
Strike all that look upon with marvel. Come;   100
I'll fill your grave up. Stir; nay, come away.
Bequeath to death your numbness, for from him
Dear life redeems you. You perceive she stirs.

[HERMIONE comes down from the pedestal.]

Start not; her actions shall be holy as
You hear my spell is lawful. Do not shun her   105
Until you see her die again; for then
You kill her double. Nay, present your hand.
When she was young you woo'd her; now in age
Is she become the suitor?

Leontes

O, she's warm!
If this be magic, let it be an art   110
Lawful as eating.

Polixenes

She embraces him.

Camillo

She hangs about his neck.
If she pertain to life, let her speak too.

Polixenes

Ay, and make it manifest where she has liv'd,
Or how stol'n from the dead.

Paulina

That she is living,   115
Were it but told you, should be hooted at

Like an old tale; but it appears she lives
Though yet she speak not. Mark a little while.
Please you to interpose, fair madam. Kneel,
120 And pray your mother's blessing. Turn, good lady;
Our Perdita is found.

Hermione
              You gods, look down,
And from your sacred vials pour your graces
Upon my daughter's head! Tell me, mine own,
Where hast thou been preserv'd? Where liv'd?
    How found
125 Thy father's court? For thou shalt hear that I,
Knowing by Paulina that the oracle
Gave hope thou wast in being, have preserv'd
Myself to see the issue.

Paulina
              There's time enough for that,
Lest they desire upon this push to trouble
130 Your joys with like relation. Go together,
You precious winners all; your exultation
Partake to every one. I, an old turtle,
Will wing me to some wither'd bough, and there
My mate, that's never to be found again,
Lament till I am lost.

Leontes
135   O peace, Paulina!
Thou shouldst a husband take by my consent,
As I by thine a wife. This is a match,
And made between's by vows. Thou hast found mine;
But how, is to be question'd; for I saw her,
140 As I thought, dead; and have, in vain, said many
A prayer upon her grave. I'll not seek far –
For him, I partly know his mind – to find thee
An honourable husband. Come, Camillo,
And take her by the hand whose worth and honesty
145 Is richly noted, and here justified
By us, a pair of kings. Let's from this place.

What! look upon my brother. Both your pardons,
That e'er I put between your holy looks
My ill suspicion. This your son-in-law,
And son unto the King, whom heavens directing,   150
Is troth-plight to your daughter. Good Paulina,
Lead us from hence where we may leisurely
Each one demand and answer to his part
Perform'd in this wide gap of time since first
We were dissever'd. Hastily lead away.   155

[Exeunt.]

Shakespeare: Words and Phrases

adapted from the Collins English Dictionary

abate 1 VERB to abate here means to lessen or diminish ❑ *There lives within the very flame of love/A kind of wick or snuff that will abate it* (*Hamlet 4.7*) 2 VERB to abate here means to shorten ❑ *Abate thy hours* (*A Midsummer Night's Dream 3.2*) 3 VERB to abate here means to deprive ❑ *She hath abated me of half my train* (*King Lear 2.4*)

abjure VERB to abjure means to renounce or give up ❑ *this rough magic I here abjure* (*Tempest 5.1*)

abroad ADV abroad means elsewhere or everywhere ❑ *You have heard of the news abroad* (*King Lear 2.1*)

abrogate VERB to abrogate means to put an end to ❑ *so it shall praise you to abrogate scurrility* (*Love's Labours Lost 4.2*)

abuse 1 NOUN abuse in this context means deception or fraud ❑ *What should this mean? Are all the rest come back?/Or is it some abuse, and no such thing?* (*Hamlet 4.7*) 2 NOUN an abuse in this context means insult or offence ❑ *I will be deaf to pleading and excuses/Nor tears nor prayers shall purchase our abuses* (*Romeo and Juliet 3.1*) 3 NOUN an abuse in this context means using something improperly ❑ *we'll digest/Th'abuse*

of distance (*Henry II Chorus*) 4 NOUN an abuse in this context means doing something which is corrupt or dishonest ❑ *Come, bring them away: if these be good people in a commonweal that do nothing but their abuses in common houses, I know no law: bring them away.* (*Measure for Measure 2.1*)

abuser NOUN the abuser here is someone who betrays, a betrayer ❑ *I … do attach thee/For an abuser of the world* (*Othello 1.2*)

accent NOUN accent here means language ❑ *In states unborn, and accents yet unknown* (*Julius Caesar 3.1*)

accident NOUN an accident in this context is an event or something that happened ❑ *think no more of this night's accidents* (*A Midsummer Night's Dream 4.1*)

accommodate VERB to accommodate in this context means to equip or to give someone the equipment to do something ❑ *The safer sense will ne'er accommodate/His master thus.* (*King Lear 4.6*)

according ADJ according means sympathetic or ready to agree ❑ *within the scope of choice/Lies*

my consent and fair according voice
(*Romeo and Juliet* 1.2)

account NOUN account often means
judgement (by God) or reckoning
❑ *No reckoning made, but sent to my
account/ With all my imperfections on
my head* (*Hamlet* 1.5)

accountant ADJ accountant here
means answerable or accountable
❑ *his offence is… /Accountant to the
law* (*Measure for Measure* 2.4)

ace NOUN ace here means one or first
referring to the lowest score on a dice
❑ *No die, but an ace, for him; for he is
but one./ Less than an ace, man; for he
is dead; he is nothing.* (*A Midsummer
Night's Dream* 5.1)

acquit VERB here acquit means to be
rid of or free of. It is related to the
verb quit ❑ *I am glad I am so acquit
of this tinderbox* (*The Merry Wives of
Windsor* 1.3)

afeard ADJ afeard means afraid or
frightened ❑ *Nothing afeard of what
thyself didst make* (*Macbeth* 1.3)

affiance NOUN affiance means
confidence or trust ❑ *O how hast
thou with jealousy infected/ The
sweetness of affiance* (*Henry V* 2.2)

affinity NOUN in this context, affinity
means important connections, or
relationships with important people
❑ *The Moor replies/ That he you hurt
is of great fame in Cyprus,/ And great
affinity* (*Othello* 3.1)

agnize VERB to agnize is an old
word that means that you recognize
or acknowledge something ❑ *I do
agnize/A natural and prompt alacrity
I find in hardness* (*Othello* 1.3)

ague NOUN an ague is a fever in
which the patient has hot and cold

shivers one after the other ❑ *This
is some monster of the isle with four
legs, who hath got … an ague* (*The
Tempest* 2.2)

alarm, alarum NOUN an alarm or
alarum is a call to arms or a signal for
soldiers to prepare to fight ❑ *Whence
cometh this alarum and the noise?*
(*Henry VI part I* 1.4)

Albion NOUN Albion is another
word for England ❑ *but I will sell my
dukedom,/ To buy a slobbery and a
dirty farm In that nook-shotten isle of
Albion* (*Henry V* 3.5)

all of all PHRASE all of all means
everything, or the sum of all things
❑ *The very all of all* (*Love's Labours
Lost* 5.1)

amend VERB amend in this context
means to get better or to heal ❑ *at
his touch… They presently amend*
(*Macbeth* 4.3)

anchor VERB if you anchor on
something you concentrate on it or
fix on it ❑ *My invention … Anchors
on Isabel* (*Measure for Measure* 2.4)

anon ADV anon was a common word
for soon ❑ *You shall see anon how the
murderer gets the love of Gonzago's
wife* (*Hamlet* 3.2)

antic 1 ADJ antic here means weird
or strange ❑ *I'll charm the air to give
a sound/ While you perform your antic
round* (*Macbeth* 4.1) 2 NOUN in
this context antic means a clown or
a strange, unattractive creature ❑ *If
black, why nature, drawing an antic,/
Made a foul blot* (*Much Ado About
Nothing* 3.1)

apace ADV apace was a common word
for quickly ❑ *Come apace* (*As You
Like It* 3.3)

apparel NOUN apparel means clothes or clothing ❑ *one suit of apparel* (*Hamlet 3.2*)

appliance NOUN appliance here means cure ❑ *Diseases desperate grown/ By desperate appliance are relieved* (*Hamlet 4.3*)

argument NOUN argument here means a topic of conversation or the subject ❑ *Why 'tis the rarest argument of wonder that hath shot out in our latter times* (*All's Well That Ends Well 2.3*)

arrant ADJ arrant means absolute, complete. It strengthens the meaning of a noun ❑ *By Fortune, that arrant whore* (*King Lear 2.4*)

arras NOUN an arras is a tapestry, a large cloth with a picture sewn on it using coloured thread ❑ *Behind the arras I'll convey myself/ To hear the process* (*Hamlet 3.3*)

art 1 NOUN art in this context means knowledge ❑ *Their malady convinces/ The great essay of art* (*Macbeth 4.3*) 2 NOUN art can also mean skill as it does here ❑ *He ... gave you such a masterly report/ For art and exercise in your defence* (*Hamlet 4.7*) 3 NOUN art here means magic ❑ *Now I want/ Spirits to enforce, art to enchant* (*The Tempest 5 Epilogue*)

assay 1 NOUN an assay was an attempt, a try ❑ *Make assay./ Bow, stubborn knees* (*Hamlet 3.3*) 2 NOUN assay can also mean a test or a trial ❑ *he hath made assay of her virtue* (*Measure for Measure 3.1*)

attend (on/upon) VERB attend on means to wait for or to expect ❑ *Tarry I here, I but attend on death* (*Two Gentlemen of Verona 3.1*)

auditor NOUN an auditor was a member of an audience or someone who listens ❑ *I'll be an auditor* (*A Midsummer Night's Dream 3.1*)

aught NOUN aught was a common word which meant anything ❑ *if my love thou holdest at aught* (*Hamlet 4.3*)

aunt 1 NOUN an aunt was another word for an old woman and also means someone who talks a lot or a gossip ❑ *The wisest aunt telling the saddest tale* (*A Midsummer Night's Dream 2.1*) 2 NOUN aunt could also mean a mistress or a prostitute ❑ *the thrush and the jay/ Are summer songs for me and my aunts/ While we lie tumbling in the hay* (*The Winter's Tale 4.3*)

avaunt EXCLAM avaunt was a common word which meant go away ❑ *Avaunt, you curs!* (*King Lear 3.6*)

aye ADV here aye means always or ever ❑ *Whose state and honour I for aye allow* (*Richard II 5.2*)

baffle VERB baffle meant to be disgraced in public or humiliated ❑ *I am disgraced, impeached, and baffled here* (*Richard II 1.1*)

bald ADJ bald means trivial or silly ❑ *I knew 'twould be a bald conclusion* (*The Comedy of Errors 2.2*)

ban NOUN a ban was a curse or an evil spell ❑ *Sometimes with lunatic bans... Enforce their charity* (*King Lear 2.3*)

barren ADJ barren meant empty or hollow ❑ *now I let go your hand, I am barren.* (*Twelfth Night 1.3*)

base ADJ base is an adjective that means unworthy or dishonourable ❑ *civet is of a baser birth than tar* (*As You Like It 3.2*)

base 1 ADJ base can also mean of low social standing or someone who was not part of the ruling class ❑ *Why brand they us with 'base'?* (*King Lear 1.2*) 2 ADJ here base means poor quality ❑ *Base cousin,/ Darest thou break first?* (*Two Noble Kinsmen 3.3*)

bawdy NOUN bawdy means obscene or rude ❑ *Bloody, bawdy villain!* (*Hamlet 2.2*)

bear in hand PHRASE bear in hand means taken advantage of or fooled ❑ *This I made good to you In our last conference, passed in probation with you/ How you were borne in hand* (*Macbeth 3.1*)

beard VERB to beard someone was to oppose or confront them ❑ *Com'st thou to beard me in Denmark?* (*Hamlet 2.2*)

beard, in one's PHRASE if you say something in someone's beard you say it to their face ❑ *I will verify as much in his beard* (*Henry V 3.2*)

beaver NOUN a beaver was a visor on a battle helmet ❑ *O yes, my lord, he wore his beaver up* (*Hamlet 1.2*)

become VERB if something becomes you it suits you or is appropriate to you ❑ *Nothing in his life became him like the leaving it* (*Macbeth 1.4*)

bed, brought to PHRASE to be brought to bed means to give birth ❑ *His wife but yesternight was brought to bed* (*Titus Andronicus 4.2*)

bedabbled ADJ if something is bedabbled it is sprinkled ❑ *Bedabbled with the dew, and torn with briers* (*A Midsummer Night's Dream 3.2*)

Bedlam NOUN Bedlam was a word used for Bethlehem Hospital which was a place the insane were sent to ❑ *The country give me proof and precedent/ Of Bedlam beggars* (*King Lear 2.3*)

bed-swerver NOUN a bed-swerver was someone who was unfaithful in marriage, an adulterer ❑ *she's/ A bed-swerver* (*Winter's Tale 2.1*)

befall 1 VERB to befall is to happen, occur or take place ❑ *In this same interlude it doth befall/ That I present a wall* (*A Midsummer Night's Dream 5.1*) 2 VERB to befall can also mean to happen to someone or something ❑ *fair befall thee and thy noble house* (*Richard III 1.3*)

behoof NOUN behoof was an advantage or benefit ❑ *All our surgeons/ Convent in their behoof* (*Two Noble Kinsmen 1.4*)

beldam NOUN a beldam was a witch or old woman ❑ *Have I not reason, beldams as you are?* (*Macbeth 3.5*)

belike ADV belike meant probably, perhaps or presumably ❑ *belike he likes it not* (*Hamlet 3.2*)

bent 1 NOUN bent means a preference or a direction ❑ *Let me work,/ For I can give his humour true bent,/ And I will bring him to the Capitol* (*Julius Caesar 2.1*) 2 ADJ if you are bent on something you are determined to do it ❑ *for now I am bent to know/ By the worst means the worst.* (*Macbeth 3.4*)

beshrew VERB beshrew meant to curse or wish evil on someone ❑ *much beshrew my manners and my pride/ If Hermia meant to say Lysander lied* (*A Midsummer Night's Dream 2.2*)

betime (s) ADV betime means early ❑ *To business that we love we rise betime* (*Antony and Cleopatra 4.4*)

bevy NOUN bevy meant type or sort, it was also used to mean company ❑ *many more of the same bevy* (*Hamlet 5.2*)

blazon VERB to blazon something meant to display or show it ❑ *that thy skill be more to blazon it* (*Romeo and Juliet 2.6*)

blind ADJ if you are blind when you do something you are reckless or do not care about the consequences ❑ *are you yet to your own souls so blind/That two you will war with God by murdering me* (*Richard III 1.4*)

bombast NOUN bombast was wool stuffing (used in a cushion for example) and so it came to mean padded out or long-winded. Here it means someone who talks a lot about nothing in particular ❑ *How now my sweet creature of bombast* (*Henry IV part I 2.4*)

bond 1 NOUN a bond is a contract or legal deed ❑ *Well, then, your bond, and let me see* (*Merchant of Venice 1.3*) 2 NOUN bond could also mean duty or commitment ❑ *I love your majesty/According to my bond* (*King Lear 1.1*)

bottom NOUN here bottom means essence, main point or intent ❑ *Now I see/The bottom of your purpose* (*All's Well That Ends Well 3.7*)

bounteously ADV bounteously means plentifully, abundantly ❑ *I prithee, and I'll pay thee bounteously* (*Twelfth Night 1.2*)

brace 1 NOUN a brace is a couple or two ❑ *Have lost a brace of kinsmen* (*Romeo and Juliet 5.3*) 2 NOUN if you are in a brace position it means you are ready ❑ *For that it stands not in such warlike brace* (*Othello 1.3*)

brand VERB to mark permanantly like the markings on cattle ❑ *the wheeled seat/Of fortunate Caesar ... branded his baseness that ensued* (*Anthony and Cleopatra 4.14*)

brave ADJ brave meant fine, excellent or splendid ❑ *O brave new world/That has such people in't* (*The Tempest 5.1*)

brine NOUN brine is sea-water ❑ *He shall drink nought brine, for I'll not show him/Where the quick freshes are* (*The Tempest 3.2*)

brow NOUN brow in this context means appearance ❑ *doth hourly grow/Out of his brows* (*Hamlet 3.3*)

burden 1 NOUN the burden here is a chorus ❑ *I would sing my song without a burden* (*As You Like It 3.2*) 2 NOUN burden means load or weight (this is the current meaning) ❑ *the scarfs and the bannerets about thee did manifoldly dissuade me from believing thee a vessel of too great a burden* (*All's Well that Ends Well 2.3*)

buttons, in one's PHRASE this is a phrase that means clear, easy to see ❑ *Tis in his buttons he will carry't* (*The Merry Wives of Windsor 3.2*)

cable NOUN cable here means scope or reach ❑ *The law ... Will give her cable* (*Othello 1.2*)

cadent ADJ if something is cadent it is falling or dropping ❑ *With cadent tears fret channels in her cheeks* (*King Lear 1.4*)

canker VERB to canker is to decay, become corrupt ❑ *And, as with age his body uglier grows,/ So his mind cankers* (*The Tempest 4.1*)

canon, from the PHRASE from the canon is an expression meaning out of order, improper ❑ *Twas from the canon* (*Coriolanus 3.1*)

cap-a-pie ADV cap-a-pie means from head to foot, completely ❑ *I am courtier cap-a-pie* (*The Winter's Tale 4.4*)

carbonadoed ADJ if something is carbonadoed it is cut or scored (scratched) with a knife ❑ *it is your carbonadoed* (*All's Well That Ends Well 4.5*)

carouse VERB to carouse is to drink at length, party ❑ *They cast their caps up and carouse together* (*Anthony and Cleopatra 4.12*)

carrack NOUN a carrack was a large old ship, a galleon ❑ *Faith, he tonight hath boarded a land-carrack* (*Othello 1.2*)

cassock NOUN a cassock here means a military cloak, long coat ❑ *half of the which dare not shake the snow from off their cassocks lest they shake themselves to pieces* (*All's Well That Ends Well 4.3*)

catastrophe NOUN catastrophe here means conclusion or end ❑ *pat he comes, like the catastrophe of the old comedy* (*King Lear 1.2*)

cautel NOUN a cautel was a trick or a deceptive act ❑ *Perhaps he loves you now/ And now no soil not cautel doth besmirch* (*Hamlet 1.2*)

celerity NOUN celerity was a common word for speed, swiftness ❑ *Hence hath offence his quick celerity/ When it is borne in high authority* (*Measure for Measure 4.2*)

chafe NOUN chafe meant anger or temper ❑ *this Herculean Roman does become/ The carriage of his chafe* (*Anthony and Cleopatra 1.3*)

chanson NOUN chanson was an old word for a song ❑ *The first row of the pious chanson will show you more* (*Hamlet 2.2*)

chapman NOUN a chapman was a trader or merchant ❑ *Not uttered by base sale of chapman's tongues* (*Love's Labours Lost 2.1*)

chaps, chops NOUN chaps (and chops) was a word for jaws ❑ *Which ne'er shook hands nor bade farewell to him/ Till he unseamed him from the nave to th' chops* (*Macbeth 1.2*)

chattels NOUN chattels were your moveable possessions. The word is used in the traditional marriage ceremony ❑ *She is my goods, my chattels* (*The Taming of the Shrew 3.3*)

chide VERB if you are chided by someone you are told off or reprimanded ❑ *Now I but chide, but I should use thee worse* (*A Midsummer Night's Dream 3.2*)

chinks NOUN chinks was a word for cash or money ❑ *he that can lay hold of her/ Shall have the chinks* (*Romeo and Juliet 1.5*)

choleric ADJ if something was called choleric it meant that they were quick to get angry ❑ *therewithal unruly waywardness that infirm and choleric years bring with them* (*King Lear 1.1*)

chuff NOUN a chuff was a miser,

someone who clings to his or her money ❑ *ye fat chuffs* (*Henry IV part I 2.2*)

cipher NOUN cipher here means nothing ❑ *Mine were the very cipher of a function* (*Measure for Measure 2.2*)

circummured ADJ circummured means that something is surrounded with a wall ❑ *He hath a garden circummured with brick* (*Measure for Measure 4.1*)

civet NOUN a civet is a type of scent or perfume ❑ *Give me an ounce of civet* (*King Lear 4.6*)

clamorous ADJ clamorous means noisy or boisterous ❑ *Be clamorous and leap all civil bounds* (*Twelfth Night 1.4*)

clangour, clangor NOUN clangour is a word that means ringing (the sound that bells make) ❑ *Like to a dismal clangour heard from far* (*Henry VI part III 2.3*)

cleave VERB if you cleave to something you stick to it or are faithful to it ❑ *Thy thoughts I cleave to* (*The Tempest 4.1*)

clock and clock, 'twixt PHRASE from hour to hour, without stopping or continuously ❑ *To weep 'twixt clock and clock* (*Cymbeline 3.4*)

close ADJ here close means hidden ❑ *Stand close; this is the same Athenian* (*A Midsummer Night's Dream 3.2*)

cloud NOUN a cloud on your face means that you have a troubled, unhappy expression ❑ *He has cloud in's face* (*Anthony and Cleopatra 3.2*)

cloy VERB if you cloy an appetite you satisfy it ❑ *Other women cloy/The*

appetites they feed (*Anthony and Cleopatra 2.2*)

cock-a-hoop, set PHRASE if you set cock-a-hoop you become free of everything ❑ *You will set cock-a-hoop* (*Romeo and Juliet 1.5*)

colours NOUN colours is a word used to describe battle-flags or banners. Sometimes we still say that we nail our colours to the mast if we are stating which team or side of an argument we support ❑ *the approbation of those that weep this lamentable divorce under her colours* (*Cymbeline 1.5*)

combustion NOUN combustion was a word meaning disorder or chaos ❑ *prophesying ... Of dire combustion and confused events* (*Macbeth 2.3*)

comely ADJ if you are or something is comely you or it is lovely, beautiful, graceful ❑ *O, what a world is this, when what is comely/Envenoms him that bears it!* (*As You Like It 2.3*)

commend VERB if you commend yourself to someone you send greetings to them ❑ *Commend me to my brother* (*Measure for Measure 1.4*)

compact NOUN a compact is an agreement or a contract ❑ *what compact mean you to have with us?* (*Julius Caesar 3.1*)

compass 1 NOUN here compass means range or scope ❑ *you would sound me from my lowest note to the top of my compass* (*Hamlet 3.2*) 2 VERB to compass here means to achieve, bring about or make happen ❑ *How now shall this be compassed?/ Canst thou bring me to the party?* (*Tempest 3.2*)

comptible ADJ comptible is an old word meaning sensitive ❏ *I am very comptible, even to the least sinister usage.* (*Twelfth Night 1.5*)

confederacy NOUN a confederacy is a group of people usually joined together to commit a crime. It is another word for a conspiracy ❏ *Lo, she is one of this confederacy!* (*A Midsummer Night's Dream 3.2*)

confound VERB if you confound something you confuse it or mix it up; it also means to stop or prevent ❏ *A million fail, confounding oath on oath.* (*A Midsummer Night's Dream 3.2*)

contagion NOUN contagion is an old word for disease or poison ❏ *hell itself breathes out/ Contagion to this world* (*Hamlet 3.2*)

contumely NOUN contumely is an old word for an insult ❏ *the proud man's contumely* (*Hamlet 3.1*)

counterfeit 1 VERB if you counterfeit something you copy or imitate it ❏ *Meantime your cheeks do counterfeit our roses* (*Henry VI part I 2.4*) 2 VERB in this context counterfeit means to pretend or make believe ❏ *I will counterfeit the bewitchment of some popular man* (*Coriolanus*)

coz NOUN coz was a shortened form of the word cousin ❏ *sweet my coz, be merry* (*As You Like It 1.2*)

cozenage NOUN cozenage is an old word meaning cheating or a deception ❏ *Thrown out his angle for my proper life,/ And with such coz'nage* (*Hamlet 5.2*)

crave VERB crave used to mean to beg or request ❏ *I crave your pardon* (*The Comedy of Errors 1.2*)

crotchet NOUN crotchets are strange ideas or whims ❏ *thou hast some strange crotchets in thy head now* (*The Merry Wives of Windsor 2.1*)

cuckold NOUN a cuckold is a man whose wife has been unfaithful to him ❏ *As there is no true cuckold but calamity* (*Twelfth Night 1.5*)

cuffs, go to PHRASE this phrase meant to fight ❏ *the player went to cuffs in the question* (*Hamlet 2.2*)

cup VERB in this context cup is a verb which means to pour drink or fill glasses with alcohol ❏ *cup us til the world go round* (*Anthony and Cleopatra 2.7*)

cur NOUN cur is an insult meaning dog and is also used to mean coward ❏ *Out, dog! out, cur! Thou drivest me past the bounds/ Of maiden's patience* (*A Midsummer Night's Dream 3.2*)

curiously ADV in this context curiously means carefully or skilfully ❏ *The sleeves curiously cut* (*The Taming of the Shrew 4.3*)

curry VERB curry means to flatter or to praise someone more than they are worth ❏ *I would curry with Master Shallow that no man could better command his servants* (*Henry IV part II 5.1*)

custom NOUN custom is a habit or a usual practice ❏ *Hath not old custom made this life more sweet/ Than that of painted pomp?* (*As You Like It 2.1*)

cutpurse NOUN a cutpurse is an old word for a thief. Men used to carry their money in small bags (purse) that hung from their belts; thieves would cut the purse from the belt and steal their money ❏ *A cutpurse of the empire and the rule* (*Hamlet 3.4*)

dainty ADJ dainty used to mean splendid, fine ❑ *Why, that's my dainty Ariel!* (*Tempest* 5.1)

dally VERB if you dally with something you play with it or tease it ❑ *They that dally nicely with words may quickly make them wanton* (*Twelfth Night* 3.1)

damask COLOUR damask is a light-red or pink colour ❑ *'Twas just the difference/Betwixt the constant red and mingled damask* (*As You Like It* 3.5)

dare 1 VERB dare means to challeng or, confront ❑ *He goes before me, and still dares me on* (*A Midsummer Night's Dream* 3.3) 2 VERB dare in this context means to present, deliver or inflict ❑ *all that fortune, death, and danger dare* (*Hamlet* 4.4)

darkly ADV darkly was used in this context to mean secretly or cunningly ❑ *I will go darkly to work with her* (*Measure for Measure* 5.1)

daw NOUN a daw was a slang term for idiot or fool (after the bird jackdaw which was famous for its stupidity) ❑ *Yea, just so much as you may take upon a knife's point and choke a daw withal* (*Much Ado About Nothing* 3.1)

debile ADJ debile meant weak or feeble ❑ *And debile minister great power* (*All's Well That Ends Well* 2.3)

deboshed ADJ deboshed was another way of saying corrupted or debauched ❑ *Men so disordered, deboshed and bold* (*King Lear* 1.4)

decoct VERB to decoct was to heat up, warm something ❑ *Can sodden water,/A drench for sur-reained jades*

... Decoct their cold blood to such valiant heat? (*Henry V* 3.5)

deep-revolving ADJ deep-revolving here uses the idea that you turn something over in your mind when you are thinking hard about it and so means deep-thinking, meditating ❑ *The deep-revolving Buckingham/No more shall be the neighbour to my counsels* (*Richard III* 4.2)

defect NOUN defect here means shortcoming or something that is not right ❑ *Being unprepared/Our will became the servant to defect* (*Macbeth* 2.1)

degree 1 NOUN degree here means rank, standing or station ❑ *Should a like language use to all degrees,/And mannerly distinguishment leave out/Betwixt the prince and beggar* (*The Winter's Tale* 2.1) 2 NOUN in this context, degree means extent or measure ❑ *her offence/Must be of such unnatural degree* (*King Lear* 1.1)

deify VERB if you deify something or someone you worship it or them as a God ❑ *all.. deifying the name of Rosalind* (*As You Like It* 3.2)

delated ADJ delated here means detailed ❑ *the scope/Of these delated articles* (*Hamlet* 1.2)

delicate ADJ if something was described as delicate it meant it was of fine quality or valuable ❑ *thou wast a spirit too delicate* (*The Tempest* 1.2)

demise VERB in this context demise means to transmit, give or convey ❑ *what state ... Canst thou demise to any child of mine?* (*Richard III* 4.4)

deplore VERB to deplore means to express with grief or sorrow ❑ *Never more/ Will I my master's tears to you deplore* (*Twelfth Night 3.1*)

depose VERB if you depose someone you make them take an oath, or swear something to be true ❑ *Depose him in the justice of his cause* (*Richard II 1.3*)

depositary NOUN a depositary is a trustee ❑ *Made you ... my depositary* (*King Lear 2.4*)

derive 1 VERB to derive means to comes from or to descend (it usually applies to people) ❑ *No part of it is mine,/ This shame derives itself from unknown loins.* (*Much Ado About Nothing 4.1*) 2 VERB if you derive something from someone you inherit it ❑ *Treason is not inherited ...Or, if we derive it from our friends/ What's that to me?* (*As You Like It 1.3*)

descry VERB to see or catch sight of ❑ *The news is true, my lord. He is descried* (*Anthony and Cleopatra 3.7*)

desert 1 NOUN desert means worth or merit ❑ *That dost in vile misproson shackle up/ My love and her desert* (*All's Well That Ends Well 2.3*) 2 ADJ desert is used here to mean lonely or isolated ❑ *if that love or gold/ Can in this desert place buy entertainment* (*As You LIke It 2.4*)

design 1 VERB to design means to indicate or point out ❑ *we shall see/ Justice design the victor's chivalry* (*Richard II 1.1*) 2 NOUN a design is a plan, an intention or an undertaking ❑ *hinder not the honour of his design* (*All's Well That Ends Well 3.6*)

designment NOUN a designment was a plan or undertaking ❑ *The desperate tempest hath so bang'd the Turks,/ That their designment halts* (*Othello 2.1*)

despite VERB despite here means to spite or attempt to thwart a plan ❑ *Only to despite them I will endeavour anything* (*Much Ado About Nothing 2.2*)

device NOUN a device is a plan, plot or trick ❑ *Excellent, I smell a device* (*Twelfth Night 2.3*)

disable VERB to disable here means to devalue or make little of ❑ *he disabled my judgement* (*As You Like It 5.4*)

discandy VERB here discandy means to melt away or dissolve ❑ *The hearts ... do discandy , melt their sweets* (*Anthony and Cleopatra 4.12*)

disciple VERB to disciple is to teach or train ❑ *He ...was/ Discipled of the bravest* (*All's Well That Ends Well 1.2*)

discommend VERB if you discommend something you criticize it ❑ *my dialect which you discommend so much* (*King Lear 2.2*)

discourse NOUN discourse means conversation, talk or chat ❑ *which part of it I'll waste/ With such discourse as I not doubt shall make it/ Go quick away* (*The Tempest 5.1*)

discover VERB discover used to mean to reveal or show ❑ *the Prince discovered to Claudio that he loved my niece* (*Much Ado About Nothing 1.2*)

disliken VERB disguise, make unlike ❑ *disliken/ The truth of your own seeming* (*The Winter's Tale 4.4*)

dismantle VERB to dismantle is to remove or take away ❑ *Commit a thing so monstrous to dismantle/*

So many folds of favour (*King Lear 1.1*)

disponge VERB disponge means to pour out or rain down ❑ *The poisonous damp of night disponge upon me* (*Anthony and Cleopatra 4.9*)

distrain VERB to distrain something is to confiscate it ❑ *My father's goods are all distrained and sold* (*Richard II 2.3*)

divers ADJ divers is an old word for various ❑ *I will give out divers schedules of my beauty* (*Twelfth Night 1.5*)

doff VERB to doff is to get rid of or dispose ❑ *make our women fight/ To doff their dire distresses* (*Macbeth 4.3*)

dog VERB if you dog someone or something you follow them or it closely ❑ *I will rather leave to see Hector than not to dog him* (*Troilus and Cressida 5.1*)

dotage NOUN dotage here means infatuation ❑ *Her dotage now I do begin to pity* (*A Midsummer NIght's Dream 4.1*)

dotard NOUN a dotard was an old fool ❑ *I speak not like a dotard nor a fool* (*Much Ado About Nothing 5.1*)

dote VERB to dote is to love, cherish, care without seeing any fault ❑ *And won her soul; and she, sweet lady, dotes,/ Devoutly dotes, dotes in idolatry* (*A Midsummer Night's Dream 1.1*)

doublet NOUN a doublet was a man's close-fitting jacket with short skirt ❑ *Lord Hamlet, with his doublet all unbraced* (*Hamlet 2.1*)

dowager NOUN a dowager is a widow ❑ *Like to a step-dame or a dowage* (*A Midsummer Night's Dream 1.1*)

dowdy NOUN a dowdy was an ugly woman ❑ *Dido was a dowdy* (*Romeo and Juliet 2.4*)

dower NOUN a dower (or dowery) is the riches or property given by the father of a bride to her husband-to-be ❑ *Thy truth then by they dower* (*King Lear 1.1*)

dram NOUN a dram is a tiny amount ❑ *Why, everything adheres together that no dram of a scruple* (*Twelfth Night 3.4*)

drift NOUN drift is a plan, scheme or intention ❑ *Shall Romeo by my letters know our drift* (*Romeo and Juliet 4.1*)

dropsied ADJ dropsied means pretentious ❑ *Where great additions swell's and virtues none/ It is a dropsied honour* (*All's Well That Ends Well 2.3*)

drudge NOUN a drudge was a slave, servant ❑ *If I be his cuckold, he's my drudge* (*All's Well That Ends Well 1.3*)

dwell VERB to dwell sometimes meant to exist, to be ❑ *I'd rather dwell in my necessity* (*Merchant of Venice 1.3*)

earnest ADJ an earnest was a pledge to pay or a payment in advance ❑ *for an earnest of a greater honour/ He bade me from him call thee Thane of Cawdor* (*Macbeth 1.3*)

ecstasy NOUN madness ❑ *This is the very ecstasy of love* (*Hamlet 2.1*)

edict NOUN law or declaration ❑ *It stands as an edict in destiny.* (*A Midsummer Night's Dream 1.1*)

egall ADJ egall is an old word meaning equal ❑ *companions/ Whose souls do bear an egall yoke of love* (*Merchant of Venice 2.4*)

eisel NOUN eisel meant vinegar ❑ *Woo't drink up eisel?* (*Hamlet 5.1*)

eke, eke out VERB eke meant to add to, to increase. Eke out nowadays means to make something last as long as possible – particularly in the sense of making money last a long time ❑ *Still be kind/ And eke out our performance with your mind* (*Henry V Chorus*)

elbow, out at PHRASE out at elbow is an old phrase meaning in poor condition – as when your jacket sleeves are worn at the elbow which shows that it is an old jacket ❑ *He cannot, sir. He's out at elbow* (*Measure for Measure 2.1*)

element NOUN elements were thought to be the things from which all things were made. They were: air, earth, water and fire ❑ *Does not our lives consist of the four elements?* (*Twelfth Night 2.3*)

elf VERB to elf was to tangle ❑ *I'll ... elf all my hairs in knots* (*King Lear 2.3*)

embassy NOUN an embassy was a message ❑ *We'll once more hear Orsino's embassy.* (*Twelfth Night 1.5*)

emphasis NOUN emphasis here means a forceful expression or strong statement ❑ *What is he whose grief/ Bears such an emphasis* (*Hamlet 5.1*)

empiric NOUN an empiric was an untrained doctor sometimes called a quack ❑ *we must not ... prostitute our past-cure malady/ To empirics* (*All's Well That Ends Well 2.1*)

emulate ADJ emulate here means envious ❑ *pricked on by a most emulate pride* (*Hamlet 1.1*)

enchant VERB to enchant meant to put a magic spell on ❑ *Damn'd as thou art, thou hast enchanted her,/ For I'll refer me to all things of sense* (*Othello 1.2*)

enclog VERB to enclog was to hinder something or to provide an obstacle to it ❑ *Traitors enscarped to enclog the guitless keel* (*Othello 1.2*)

endure VERB to endure was to allow or to permit ❑ *and will endure/ Our setting down before't.* (*Macbeth 5.4*)

enfranchise VERB if you enfranchised something you set it free ❑ *Do this or this;/ Take in that kingdom and enfranchise that;/ Perform't, or else we damn thee.'* (*Anthony and Cleopatra 1.1*)

engage VERB to engage here means to pledge or to promise ❑ *This to be true I do engage my life* (*As You Like It 5.4*)

engaol VERB to lock up or put in prison ❑ *Within my mouth you have engaoled my tongue* (*Richard II 1.3*)

engine NOUN an engine was a plot, device or a machine ❑ *their promises, enticements, oaths, tokens, and all these engines, of lust, are not the things they go under* (*All's Well That Ends Well 3.5*)

englut VERB if you were engulfed you were swallowed up or eaten whole ❑ *For certainly thou art so near the gulf,/ Thou needs must be englutted.* (*Henry V 4.3*)

enjoined ADJ enjoined describes people joined together for the same reason ❑ *Of enjoined penitents/*

There's four or five (*All's Well That Ends Well 3.5*)

entertain 1 VERB to entertain here means to welcome or receive ❏ *Approach, rich Ceres, her to entertain.* (*The Tempest 4.1*) 2 VERB to entertain in this context means to cherish, hold in high regard or to respect ❏ *and I quake,/ Lest thou a feverous life shouldst entertain/ And six or seven winters more respect/ Than a perpetual honour.* (*Measure for Measure 3.1*) 3 VERB to entertain means to give something consideration ❏ *But entertain it,/ And though you think me poor, I am the man/ Will give thee all the world.* (*Anthony and Cleopatra 2.7*) 4 VERB to entertain here means to treat or handle ❏ *your highness is not entertained with that ceremonious affection as you were wont* (*King Lear 1.4*)

envious ADJ envious meant spiteful or vindictive ❏ *he shall appear to the envious a scholar* (*Measure for Measure 3.2*)

ere PREP ere was a common word for before ❏ *ere this I should ha' fatted all the region kites* (*Hamlet 2.2*)

err VERB to err means to go astray, to make a mistake ❏ *And as he errs, doting on Hermia's eyes* (*A Midsummer Night's Dream 1.1*)

erst ADV erst was a common word for once or before ❏ *that erst brought sweetly forth/ The freckled cowslip* (*Henry V 5.2*)

eschew VERB if you eschew something you deliberately avoid doing it ❏ *What cannot be eschewed must be embraced* (*The Merry Wives of Windsor 5.5*)

escote VERB to escote meant to pay for, support ❏ *How are they escoted?* (*Hamlet 2.2*)

estimable ADJ estimable meant appreciative ❏ *I could not with such estimable wonder over-far believe that* (*Twelfth Night 2.1*)

extenuate VERB extenuate means to lessen ❏ *Which by no means we may extenuate* (*A Midsummer Night's Dream 1.1*)

fain ADV fain was a common word meaning gladly or willingly ❏ *I would fain prove so* (*Hamlet 2.2*)

fall NOUN in a voice or music fall meant going higher and lower ❏ *and so die/ That strain again! it had a dying fall* (*Twelfth Night 1.1*)

false ADJ false was a common word for treacherous ❏ *this is counter, you false Danish dogs!* (*Hamlet 4.5*)

fare VERB fare means to get on or manage ❏ *I fare well* (*The Taming of the Shrew Introduction 2*)

feign VERB to feign was to make up, pretend or fake ❏ *It is the more like to be feigned* (*Twelfth Night 1.5*)

fie EXCLAM fie was an exclamation of disgust ❏ *Fie, that you'll say so!* (*Twelfth Night 1.3*)

figure VERB to figure was to symbolize or look like ❏ *Wings and no eyes, figure unheedy haste* (*A Midsummer Night's Dream 1.1*)

filch VERB if you filch something you steal it ❏ *With cunning hast thou filch'd my daughter's heart* (*A Midsummer Night's Dream 1.1*)

flout VERB to flout something meant to scorn it ❏ *Why will you suffer her to flout me thus?* (*A Midsummer Night's Dream 3.2*)

fond ADJ fond was a common word meaning foolish ❏ *Shall we their fond pageant see?* (*A Midsummer Night's Dream 3.2*)

footing 1 NOUN footing meant landing on shore, arrival, disembarkation ❏ *Whose footing here anticipates our thoughts/A se'nnight's speed.* (*Othello 2.1*) 2 NOUN footing also means support ❏ *there your charity would have lacked footing* (*Winter's Tale 3.3*)

forsooth ADV in truth, certainly, truly
❏ *I had rather, forsooth, go before you like a man* (*The Merry Wives of Windsor 3.2*)

forswear VERB if you forswear you lie, swear falsely or break your word ❏ *he swore a thing to me on Monday night, which he forswore on Tuesday morning* (*Much Ado About Nothing 5.1*)

freshes NOUN a fresh is a fresh water stream ❏ *He shall drink nought brine, for I'll not show him/Where the quick freshes are.* (*Tempest 3.2*)

furlong NOUN a furlong is a measure of distance. It is the equivalent on one eight of a mile ❏ *Now would I give a thousand furlongs of sea for an acre of barren ground* (*Tempest 1.1*)

gaberdine NOUN a gaberdine is a cloak ❏ *My best way is to creep under his gaberdine* (*Tempest 2.2*)

gage NOUN a gage was a challenge to duel or fight ❏ *There is my gage, Aumerle, in gage to thine* (*Richard II 4.1*)

gait NOUN your gait is your way of walking or step ❏ *I know her by her gait* (*Tempest 4.1*)

gall VERB to gall is to annoy or irritate ❏ *Let it not gall your patience, good Iago,/That I extend my manners* (*Othello 2.1*)

gambol NOUN frolic or play ❏ *Hop in his walks, and gambol in his eyes* (*A Midsummer Night's Dream 3.1*)

gaskins NOUN gaskins is an old word for trousers ❏ *or, if both break, your gaskins fall.* (*Twelfth Night 1.5*)

gentle ADJ gentle means noble or well-born ❏ *thrice-gentle Cassio!* (*Othello 3.4*)

glass NOUN a glass was another word for a mirror ❏ *no woman's face remember/Save from my glass, mine own* (*Tempest 3.1*)

gleek VERB to gleek means to make a joke or jibe ❏ *Nay, I can gleek upon occasion* (*A Midsummer Night's Dream 3.1*)

gust NOUN gust meant taste, desire or enjoyment. We still say that if you do something with gusto you do it with enjoyment or enthusiasm ❏ *the gust he hath in quarrelling* (*Twelfth Night 1.3*)

habit NOUN habit means clothes ❏ *You know me by my habit* (*Henry V 3.6*)

heaviness NOUN heaviness means sadness or grief ❏ *So sorrow's heaviness doth heavier grow/For debt that bankrupt sleep doth sorrow owe* (*A Midsummer Night's Dream 3.2*)

heavy ADJ if you are heavy you are said to be sad or sorrowful ❏ *Away from light steals home my heavy son* (*Romeo and Juliet 1.1*)

hie VERB to hie meant to hurry ❏ *My husband hies him home* (*All Well That Ends Well 4.4*)

hollowly ADV if you did something hollowly you did it insincerely ❏ *If hollowly invert/What best is boded me to mischief!* (*Tempest 3.1*)

holy-water, court PHRASE if you court holy water you make empty promises, or make statements which sound good but have no real meaning ❏ *court holy-water in a dry house is better than this rain-water out o'door* (*King Lear 3.2*)

howsoever ADV howsoever was often used instead of however ❏ *But howsoever strange and admirable* (*A Midsummer Night's Dream 5.1*)

humour NOUN your humour was your mood, frame of mind or temperament ❏ *it fits my humour well* (*As You Like It 3.2*)

ill ADJ ill means bad ❏ *I must thank him only,/ Let my remembrance suffer ill report* (*Antony and Cleopatra 2.2*)

indistinct ADJ inseparable or unable to see a difference ❏ *Even till we make the main and the aerial blue/An indistinct regard.* (*Othello 2.1*)

indulgence NOUN indulgence meant approval ❏ *As you from crimes would pardoned be,/ Let your indulgence set me free* (*The Tempest Epilogue*)

infirmity NOUN infirmity was weakness or fraility ❏ *Be not disturbed with my infirmity* (*The Tempest 4.1*)

intelligence NOUN here intelligence means information ❏ *Pursue her; and for this intelligence/ If I have thanks* (*A Midsummer Night's Dream 1.1*)

inwards NOUN inwards meant someone's internal organs ❏ *the thought whereof/ Doth like a poisonous mineral gnaw my inwards* (*Othello 2.1*)

issue 1 NOUN the issue of a marriage are the children ❏ *To thine and Albany's issues,/ Be this perpetual* (*King Lear 1.1*) 2 NOUN in this context issue means outcome or result ❏ *I am to pray you, not to strain my speech,/ To grosser issues* (*Othello*)

kind NOUN kind here means situation or case ❏ *But in this kind, wanting your father's voice,/ The other must be held the worthier.* (*A Midsummer Night's Dream 1.1*)

knave NOUN a knave was a common word for scoundrel ❏ *How absolute the knave is!* (*Hamlet 5.1*)

league NOUN A distance. A league was the distance a person could walk in one hour ❏ *From Athens is her house remote seven leagues* (*A Midsummer Night's Dream 1.1*)

lief, had as ADJ I had as lief means I should like just as much ❏ *I had as lief the town crier spoke my lines* (*Hamlet 1.2*)

livery NOUN livery was a costume, outfit, uniform usually worn by a servant ❏ *You can endure the livery of a nun* (*A Midsummer Night's Dream 1.1*)

loam NOUN loam is soil containing decayed vegetable matter and therefore good for growing crops and plants ❏ *and let him have some plaster, or some loam, or some rough-cast about him, to signify wall* (*A Midsummer Night's Dream 3.1*)

lusty ADJ lusty meant strong ❏ *and oared/Himself with his good arms in lusty stroke/ To th' shore* (*The Tempest 2.1*)

maidenhead NOUN maidenhead means chastity or virginity ❑ *What I am, and what I would, are as secret as maidenhead* (*Twelfth Night 1.5*)

mark VERB mark means to note or pay attention to ❑ *Where sighs and groans,/ Are made not marked* (*Macbeth 4.3*)

marvellous ADJ very or extremely ❑ *here's a marvellous convenient place for our rehearsal* (*A Midsummer Night's Dream 3.1*)

meet ADJ right or proper ❑ *tis most meet you should* (*Macbeth 5.1*)

merely ADV completely or entirely ❑ *Love is merely a madness* (*As You Like It 3.2*)

misgraffed ADJ misgraffed is an old word for mismatched or unequal ❑ *Or else misgraffed in respect of years* (*A Midsummer Night's Dream 1.1*)

misprision NOUN a misprision meant an error or mistake ❑ *Misprision in the highest degree!* (*Twelfth Night 1.5*)

mollification NOUN mollification is appeasement or a way of preventing someone getting angry ❑ *I am to hull here a little longer. Some mollification for your giant* (*Twelfth Night 1.5*)

mouth, cold in the PHRASE a well-known saying of the time which meant to be dead ❑ *What, must our mouths be cold?* (*The Tempest 1.1*)

murmur NOUN murmur was another word for rumour or hearsay ❑ *and then 'twas fresh in murmur* (*Twelfth Night 1.2*)

murrain NOUN murrain was another word for plague, pestilence ❑ *A murrain on your monster, and the devil take your fingers!* (*The Tempest 3.2*)

neaf NOUN neaf meant fist ❑ *Give me your neaf, Monsieur Mustardseed* (*A Midsummer Night's Dream 4.1*)

nice 1 ADJ nice had a number of meanings here it means fussy or particular ❑ *An therefore, goaded with most sharp occasions,/ Which lay nice manners by, I put you to/ The use of your own virtues* (*All's Well That Ends Well 5.1*) 2 ADJ nice here means critical or delicate ❑ *We're good… To set so rich a man/ On the nice hazard of one doubtful hour?* (*Henry IV part 1*) 3 ADJ nice in this context means carefully accurate, fastidious ❑ *O relation/ Too nice and yet too true!* (*Macbeth 4.3*) 4 ADJ trivial, unimportant ❑ *Romeo .. Bid him bethink/ How nice the quarrel was* (*Romeo and Juliet 3.1*)

nonpareil NOUN if you are nonpareil you are without equal, peerless ❑ *though you were crown'd/ The nonpareil of beauty!* (*Twelfth Night 1.5*)

office NOUN office here means business or work ❑ *Speak your office* (*Twelfth Night 1.5*)

outsport VERB outsport meant to overdo ❑ *Let's teach ourselves that honorable stop,/ Not to outsport discretion.* (*Othello 2.2*)

owe VERB owe meant own, possess ❑ *Lend less than thou owest* (*King Lear 1.4*)

paragon 1 VERB to paragon was to surpass or excede ❑ *he hath achieved a maid/ That paragons description and wild fame* (*Othello 2.1*) 2 VERB to paragon could also mean to compare with ❑ *I will give thee* *bloody teeth If thou with Caesar paragon again/My man of men (Anthony and Cleopatra 1.5)*

pate NOUN pate is another word for head ❏ *Back, slave, or I will break thy pate across (The Comedy of Errors 2.1)*

paunch VERB to paunch someone is to stab (usually in the stomach). Paunch is still a common word for a stomach ❏ *Batter his skull, or paunch him with a stake (The Tempest 3.2)*

peevish ADJ if you are peevish you are irritable or easily angered ❏ *Run after that same peevish messenger (Twelfth Night 1.5)*

peradventure ADV perhaps or maybe ❏ *Peradventure this is not Fortune's work (As You Like It 1.2)*

perforce 1 ADV by force or violently ❏ *my rights and royalties,/ Plucked from my arms perforce (Richard II 2.3)* 2 ADV necessarily ❏ *The hearts of men, they must perforce have melted (Richard II 5.2)*

personage NOUN personage meant your appearance ❏ *Of what personage and years is he? (Twelfth Night 1.5)*

pestilence NOUN pestilence was a common word for plague or disease ❏ *Methought she purg'd the air of pestilence! (Twelfth Night 1.1)*

physic NOUN physic was medicine or a treatment ❏ *'tis a physic/That's bitter to sweet end (Measure for Measure 4.6)*

place NOUN place means a person's position or rank ❏ *Sons, kinsmen, thanes,/And you whose places are the nearest (Macbeth 1.4)*

post NOUN here a post means a messenger ❏ *there are twenty weak and wearied posts/Come from the north (Henry IV part II 2.4)*

pox NOUN pox was a word for any disease during which the victim had blisters on the skin. It was also a curse, a swear word ❏ *The pox of such antic, lisping, affecting phantasims (Romeo and Juliet 2.4)*

prate VERB to prate means to chatter ❏ *if thou prate of mountains (Hamlet 5.1)*

prattle VERB to prattle is to chatter or talk without purpose ❏ *I prattle out of fashion, and I dote In mine own comforts (Othello 2.1)*

precept NOUN a precept was an order or command ❏ *and my father's precepts I therein do forget. (The Tempest 3.1)*

present ADJ present here means immediate ❏ *We'll put the matter to the present push (Hamlet 5.1)*

prithee EXCLAM prithee is the equivalent of please or may I ask – a polite request ❏ *I prithee, and I'll pay thee bounteously (Twelfth Night 1.2)*

prodigal NOUN a prodigal is someone who wastes or squanders money ❏ *he's a very fool, and a prodigal (Twelfth Night 1.3)*

purpose NOUN purpose is used here to mean intention ❏ *understand my purposes aright (King Lear 1.4)*

quaff VERB quaff was a common word which meant to drink heavily or take a big drink ❏ *That quaffing and drinking will undo you (Twelfth Night 1.3)*

quaint 1 ADJ clever, ingenious ❏ *with a quaint device* (*The Tempest 3.3*) 2 ADJ cunning ❏ *I'll… tell quaint lies* (*Merchant of Venice 3.4*) 3 ADJ pretty, attractive ❏ *The clamorous owl, that nightly hoots and wonders/At our quaint spirit* (*A Midsummer Night's Dream 2.2*)

quoth VERB an old word which means say ❏ *'Tis dinner time.' quoth I* (*The Comedy of Errors 2.1*)

rack NOUN a rack described clouds or a cloud formation ❏ *And, like this insubstantial pageant faded,/ Leave not a rack behind* (*The Tempest 4.1*)

rail VERB to rant or swear at. It is still used occasionally today ❏ *Why do I rail on thee* (*Richard II 5.5*)

rate NOUN rate meant estimate, opinion ❏ *My son is lost, and, in my rate, she too* (*The Tempest 2.1*)

recreant NOUN recreant is an old word which means coward ❏ *Come, recreant, come, thou child* (*A Midsummer Night's Dream 3.2*)

remembrance NOUN remembrance is used here to mean memory or recollection ❏ *our remembrances of days foregone* (*All's Well That Ends Well 1.3*)

resolute ADJ firm or not going to change your mind ❏ *You are resolute, then?* (*Twelfth Night 1.5*)

revels NOUN revels means celebrations or a party ❏ *Our revels now are ended* (*The Tempest 4.1*)

rough-cast NOUN a mixture of lime and gravel (sometimes shells too) for use on an outer wall ❏ *and let him have some plaster, or some loam, or some rough-cast about him, to signify wall* (*A Midsummer Night's Dream 3.1*)

sack NOUN sack was another word for wine ❏ *My man-monster hath drowned his tongue in sack.* (*The Tempest 3.2*)

sad ADJ in this context sad means serious, grave ❏ *comes me the Prince and Claudio… in sad conference* (*Much Ado About Nothing 1.3*)

sampler NOUN a piece of embroidery, which often showed the family tree ❏ *Both on one sampler, sitting on one cushion* (*A Midsummer Night's Dream 3.2*)

saucy ADJ saucy means rude ❏ *I heard you were saucy at my gates* (*Twelfth Night 1.5*)

schooling NOUN schooling means advice ❏ *I have some private schooling for you both.* (*A Midsummer Night's Dream 1.1*)

seething ADJ seething in this case means boiling – we now use seething when we are very angry ❏ *Lovers and madmen have such seething brains* (*A Midsummer Night's Dream 5.1*)

semblative ADJ semblative means resembling or looking like ❏ *And all is semblative a woman's part.* (*Twelfth Night 1.4*)

several ADJ several here means separate or different ❏ *twenty several messengers* (*Anthony and Cleopatra 1.5*)

shrew NOUN An annoying person or someone who makes you cross ❏ *Bless you, fair shrew.* (*Twelfth Night 1.3*)

shroud VERB to shroud is to hide or shelter ❑ *I will here, shroud till the dregs of the storm be past* (*The Tempest* 2.2)

sickleman NOUN a sickleman was someone who used a sickle to harvest crops ❑ *You sunburnt sicklemen, of August weary* (*The Tempest* 4.1)

soft ADV soft here means wait a moment or stop ❑ *But, soft, what nymphs are these* (*A Midsummer Night's Dream* 4.1)

something ADV something here means somewhat or rather ❑ *Be something scanter of your maiden presence* (*Hamlet* 1.3)

sooth NOUN truly ❑ *Yes, sooth; and so do you* (*A Midsummer Night's Dream* 3.2)

spleen NOUN spleen means fury or anger ❑ *That, in a spleen, unfolds both heaven and earth* (*A Midsummer Night's Dream* 1.1)

sport NOUN sport means recreation or entertainment ❑ *I see our wars/ Will turn unto a peaceful comic sport* (*Henry VI part I* 2.2)

strain NOUN a strain is a tune or a musical phrase ❑ *and so die/ That strain again! it had a dying fall* (*Twelfth Night* 1.1)

suffer VERB in this context suffer means perish or die ❑ *but an islander that hath lately suffered by a thunderbolt.* (*The Tempest* 2.2)

suit NOUN a suit is a petition, request or proposal (marriage) ❑ *Because she will admit no kind of suit* (*Twelfth Night* 1.2)

sup VERB to sup is to have supper ❑ *Go know of Cassio where he supped tonight* (*Othello* 5.1)

surfeit NOUN a surfeit is an amount which is too large ❑ *If music be the food of love, play on;/ Give me excess of it, that, surfeiting,/ The appetite may sicken* (*Twelfth Night* 1.1)

swain NOUN a swain is a suitor or person who wants to marry ❑ *take this transformed scalp/ From off the head of this Athenian swain* (*A Midsummer Night's Dream* 4.1)

thereto ADV thereto meant also ❑ *If she be black, and thereto have a wit* (*Othello* 2.1)

throstle NOUN a throstle was a name for a song-bird ❑ *The throstle with his note so true* (*A Midsummer Night's Dream* 3.1)

tidings NOUN tidings meant news ❑ *that upon certain tidings now arrived, importing the mere perdition of the Turkish fleet* (*Othello* 2.2)

transgress VERB if you transgress you break a moral law or rule of behaviour ❑ *Virtue that transgresses is but patched with sin* (*Twelfth Night* 1.5)

troth, by my PHRASE this phrase means I swear or in truth or on my word ❑ *By my troth, Sir Toby, you must come in earlier o' nights* (*Twelfth Night* 1.3)

trumpery NOUN trumpery means things that look expensive but are worth nothing (often clothing) ❑ *The trumpery in my house, go bring it hither/ For stale catch these thieves* (*The Tempest* 4.1)

twink NOUN In the wink of an eye or no time at all ❑ *Ay, with a twink* (*The Tempest* 4.1)

undone ADJ if something or someone is undone they are ruined, destroyed, brought down ❑ *You have undone a man of fourscore three* (*The Winter's Tale 4.4*)

varlets NOUN varlets were villains or ruffians ❑ *Say again: where didst thou leave these varlets?* (*The Tempest 4.1*)

vaward NOUN the vaward is an old word for the vanguard, front part or earliest ❑ *And since we have the vaward of the day* (*A Midsummer Night's Dream 4.1*)

visage NOUN face ❑ *when Phoebe doth behold/Her silver visage in the watery glass* (*A Midsummer Night's Dream 1.1*)

voice NOUN voice means vote ❑ *He has our voices* (*Coriolanus 2.3*)

waggish ADJ waggish means playful ❑ *As waggish boys in game themselves forswear* (*A Midsummer Night's Dream 1.1*)

wane VERB to wane is to vanish, go down or get slighter. It is most often used to describe a phase of the moon ❑ *but, O, methinks, how slow/This old moon wanes* (*A Midsummer Night's Dream 1.1*)

want VERB to want means to lack or to be without ❑ *a beast that wants discourse of reason/Would have mourned longer* (*Hamlet 1.2*)

warrant VERB to assure, promise, guarantee ❑ *I warrant your grace* (*As You Like It 1.2*)

welkin NOUN welkin is an old word for the sky or the heavens ❑ *The starry welkin cover thou anon/With drooping fog as black as Acheron* (*A Midsummer Night's Dream 3.2*)

wench NOUN wench is an old word for a girl ❑ *Well demanded, wench* (*The Tempest 1.2*)

whence ADV from where ❑ *Whence came you, sir?* (*Twelfth Night 1.5*)

wherefore ADV why ❑ *Wherefore, sweetheart? what's your metaphor?* (*Twelfth Night 1.3*)

wide-chopped ADJ if you were wide-chopped you were big-mouthed ❑ *This wide-chopped rascal* (*The Tempest 1.1*)

wight NOUN wight is an old word for person or human being ❑ *She was a wight, if ever such wight were* (*Othello 2.1*)

wit NOUN wit means intelligence or wisdom ❑ *thou didst conclude hairy men plain dealers, without wit* (*The Comedy of Errors 2.2*)

wits NOUN wits mean mental sharpness ❑ *we that have good wits have much to answer for* (*As You Like It 4.1*)

wont ADJ to wont is to be in the habit of doing something regularly ❑ *When were you wont to use my sister thus?* (*The Comedy of Errors 2.2*)

wooer NOUN a wooer is a suitor, someone who is hoping to marry ❑ *and of a foolish knight that you brought in one night here to be her wooer* (*Twelfth Night 1.3*)

wot VERB wot is an old word which means know or learn ❑ *for well I wot/Thou runnest before me* (*A Midsummer Night's Dream 3.2*)